**Readings in
Biblical Morality**

PRENTICE-HALL, INC., *London*
PRENTICE-HALL OF AUSTRALIA, PTY. LTD., *Sydney*
PRENTICE-HALL OF CANADA, LTD., *Toronto*
PRENTICE-HALL OF INDIA (PRIVATE) LTD., *New Delhi*
PRENTICE-HALL OF JAPAN, INC., *Tokyo*

C. LUKE SALM, F.S.C.

Chairman, Department of Theology, Manhattan College

81775

BJ1249
.S17

Readings in
Biblical Morality

Prentice-Hall, Inc. *Englewood Cliffs, New Jersey*

Nihil obstat:
    Daniel V. Flynn, J.C.D.
    CENSOR LIBRORUM
Imprimatur:
    ✠ Terence J. Cooke, D.D., V.G.

June 30, 1966

The *nihil obstat* and *imprimatur* are official declarations that a book or pamphlet is free of doctrinal or moral error. No implication is contained therein that those who have granted the *nihil obstat* and *imprimatur* agree with the contents, opinions, or statements expressed.

LIBRARY OF CONGRESS CATALOG CARD NO.: 67-10317
PRINTED IN THE UNITED STATES OF AMERICA: 75560-C
CURRENT PRINTING (LAST DIGIT):

10   9   8   7   6   5   4   3   2   1

Preface

These are days of renewal and reform in the Church. The magnificent achievements of Vatican II which crystalized that renewal and gave it definition were due largely to the renewal in biblical, liturgical, and theological studies in general that preceded the convening of the Council. Though it has been widely acknowledged that a similar renewal is overdue in the field of moral theology and though some notable attempts have been made in that direction, much preliminary and scholarly work must yet be done before a thoroughgoing revision of our moral treatises can be effected. Meanwhile, there is increasing dissatisfaction with the traditional sin-centered and casuistic manuals of morality and ethics. It seems opportune, then, to offer to the generally educated but nonprofessional public the opportunity to gain knowledge of some contemporary attempts to approach moral issues from a rather different point of view.

The theology of Vatican II is characterized by a "return to the sources." The Council documents, in their concern for contemporary relevance, reflect little of the post-Tridentine scholastic manuals. However, these documents are also conscious of a sense of continuing tradition, of a "catholic" spirit deeply rooted in the past. This combination of existential concreteness and respect for tradition is successfully balanced in the decrees of the Council through the extensive use of the tone and vocabulary of Sacred Scripture. The Fathers of the Council found in this inspired source the most authentic statement of Christian values and the elements of a profound and even revolutionary adaptation. Although the field of moral theology as such is not prominently featured in the Council documents, the Council has given an example that cannot be ignored. The studies in biblical morality that comprise this collection illustrate how the field of moral theology can pursue its own reform in the spirit of the Council.

In the same spirit, the choice of articles for this collection attempts to balance the traditional and the new, the scholarly and the popular, the documented study and the short but insightful essay. Thus anyone trained in traditional moral theology will find here chapter headings that are very familiar: Sin, Law, Commandment, Justice, Prudence, and the like. On the other hand, the analysis of these concepts in the individual articles can offer some surprising and fresh insights into the biblical meaning of a standardized vocabulary. The danger of novelty for its own sake is avoided by the solid scriptural foundation on which each author bases his presentation. For this reason, too, the collection has an ecumenical dimension, highlighting the common tradition of morality that all Christians have in the Bible, and an "ecumenical epilogue" has been appended to make this aspect of the renewal of moral teaching more explicit.

This collection is not intended primarily for the professional or the research scholar. Accordingly, the footnotes of the original essays have in most cases been considerably reduced, especially where references are made to very technical or foreign works not usually available to the general reader or student. Footnotes have been retained, however, where they would serve as a source of useful bibliography, where they further explain or elaborate some point made by the author, or where the sense of a passage or scholarly integrity obviously demands the citation of a source.

The editor is grateful to the publishers and learned societies that gave their gracious permission to reproduce these valuable materials. The authors of the articles especially deserve great thanks and praise for the vision of their scholarship and their willingness to share the results of their work with a wider audience. The Confraternity of Christian Doctrine translation of the Sacred Scripture has been used in the introductory sections and generally throughout the volume, except in cases where the authors have preferred some other version in the texts of their essays; this permission is gratefully acknowledged.

C. LUKE SALM, F.S.C.

Contents

IV. JUSTICE

V. WISDOM

VI. LAW

VII. FREEDOM

VIII. FORGIVENESS

Readings in
Biblical Morality

C. LUKE SALM, F.S.C.

Introduction to Biblical Morality

The Christian approach to morality has always featured a biblical element. Catechisms and weighty theological tomes alike have organized their moral teaching around the Ten Commandments, and treatises on the Christian life frequently take the form of a commentary on the Beatitudes. Above all, the vivid examples of concrete moral living that the rich personalities of Scripture provide have always been used to illustrate the best moral effort of man facing God: the faith of Abraham, the integrity of Joseph, the piety of David, the wisdom of Solomon, the faith-crisis of Job. The New Testament epitomizes morality in the life and teaching of Christ. The word pictures that his parables present are very familiar: the good Samaritan, the prodigal son, the proud Pharisee, the unjust steward, the rich young man, the wise virgins. Since the Church in her Liturgy presents these personalities and these parables for public proclamation and personal response, we can say that the liturgical cycle itself comprises a kind of biblical morality.

Biblical morality can also be understood in a more restricted and scientific sense as an aspect of biblical theology. Biblical morality in these terms would demand that the whole structure of scientific moral teaching be developed in terms and categories derived from Sacred Scripture. This has not been the approach of the standard moral treatises written within the context of a generally scholastic system of theology. These treatises tend to take scholastic ethics as their starting point and so, using human reason, try to systematize and illuminate the revealed norms of human behavior in more or less philosophical terms. Thus we have treatises on the ultimate end of man, human acts, law and conscience as objective and subjective

1

norms, sin and virtue, and finally a detailed examination of specific norms of behavior derived often from definitions of the theological and moral virtues. Mere illustrations from biblical sources grafted onto such a structure are hardly sufficient to justify calling the result biblical morality. Most of the inspired Scripture was written in a Semitic context and with Semitic thought patterns. More important, the vivid religious faith that the authors of Scripture had in the reality of their encounter with God gave a totally different orientation to their moral outlook. A systematic biblical theology in the field of morality will necessarily reflect this special vocabulary, structure, and emphasis.

The fact is that a fully developed biblical morality does not yet exist. Enough has been done in recent scriptural studies to sketch only the main lines of such a structure. The dialogue and covenant structure of God's plan of salvation as the Bible presents it provides a possible principle of organization. The New Testament teaching on Christian liberty supplies an important principle of action. The biblical understanding of commandment, sin, faith, justice, love, forgiveness, wisdom, and prudence could help fill in the situational specifics. Some of this vocabulary, of course, is to be found also in the scholastic treatises. Within the context of a totally biblical structure, however, they assume a different position and a new importance. Here the master concepts would seem to be salvation, covenant, and liberty. Moral norms are derived from God's love and his justice, man's response in faith and his willingness to be in God's image, the fullness of God's revelation in Christ, and the life of the Christian responsive to the inner norm of the Spirit.

Salvation in the Scripture, as the word itself suggests, is God's plan to rescue man *from* an unfortunate predicament *for* a total self-fulfillment. In its negative aspect, man's need for salvation stems from the fact of failure, the man-originated problem of evil, the human condition of sin, ignorance, distress, sickness, and death. In its positive aspect, salvation demands a transcendent source of self-fulfillment. Human plans to eliminate or mitigate evil and to provide fulfillment offer a salvation of sorts; science and culture, for example, social reform, humanitarianism, internationalism, all work toward good in an earthly context. Yet none of these human solutions is sufficiently radical or permanent. The Bible reveals how the initiative of God's love works in human history to provide man with salvation from all moral and physical failure through self-fulfillment in union with the divine. Both aspects are concretely seen in the resurrection of the man Jesus to a glorified existence, victorious over sin and death, completely fulfilled and transformed.

"Covenant" is the word that Scripture uses to describe the structure of God's plan and the commitment it demands on both sides. God takes the initiative to save man. He reveals himself to man, asks for man's free response, opens up gradually to man the various stages in the working out of the plan in man's history. Thus the covenant dimension of God's plan of salvation makes it historical, personal, and social. Each of these aspects has important implications for the development of a biblical morality.

Because God's plan is historical, because he reveals himself as Lord of history, because salvation history is the result of his initiative and love, the Judaeo-Christian religion is not a system or a cycle. We do not save ourselves by behaving ourselves. There is no plan of ascesis, meditation, or any other merely human effort that of itself can lead us to the divine. It is truer to say that God saves us in spite of ourselves, in spite of our failure, in spite of the weakness of our response. The blindness and indifference of men simply cannot halt the forward march of God's plan in human history. Despite infidelity, idolatry, apostasy, and despair, God himself becomes one of us, "joins the human race," so to speak, and in the person of his Son takes on our human frailty. In his transition from death and total human failure to the glory of resurrected life, the man Jesus, who is God, wins glory for himself and salvation for all men. Having given freedom from sin and death, the resurrection means for Christ and for the Christian a new freedom in a new life. Thus the culmination of salvation history is at the same time the epitome of its moral teaching. The resurrection is the source of the sending of the Spirit and of that grace by which we conquer sin and failure of every kind and enter into fulfillment in the very life of God.

The structure of covenant morality is highly personal. Salvation is the work of God's personal initiative. He does not effect it arbitrarily from afar or from above. He reveals himself to man in his power to save, in his covenant love, and in his sacred name. Astonishingly, he becomes personally available to us in the person of his Son. Furthermore, he asks for a free human response. He will not save free men against their will. He invites us in his loving grace to open ourselves to the action of his plan and so confers a dignity upon us that is more than human. No room here for the automatic, the routine, the impersonal, the unconcerned. The word we have that best sums up the biblical doctrine of God's personal initiative is *love;* *faith,* understood as total openness, the saying of a big "Amen" or "Yes!" to God, is the best we can do to summarize our personal response. Thus the personal dialogue of God's love and man's faith provides the framework and motivation for all the practical standards that man will want to adopt to govern his behavior.

To say that covenant morality is personal does not mean that it is individualistic. Quite the contrary. The Bible is well aware that the source of human failure is most often as much a breakdown in interpersonal integrity as in personal integrity. This is the point of the Cain and Abel story as well as that of the tower of Babel: men kill one another; men cannot communicate. God's remedy then must be interpersonal, too. Accordingly, his revelation of himself coincides with the formation of a people that will be his own holy people, the salvation community. From the beginning of the working of God's plan, men have had to learn that their salvation in God involves dependence upon and relation to other people. "There is no salvation outside the Church" might be paraphrased to read "There is no salvation apart from other people," specifically the people of God. That is why the New Testament presents Jesus as the New Israel and the Christian Church as the Body of Christ. There is no authentic biblical morality that does not make central this social relationship of persons united to one another in the faith-response of their common salvation.

The operational principle of biblical morality, the absolutely necessary climate of the totally Christian response, is described in the New Testament in terms of the liberty of the sons of God. When the Christian participates through baptism in the passage of Christ from death to resurrection, he dies once for all to sin and so also to the law. The Christian knows through faith and experience where salvation is and where it is not to be had. It is not to be had in a pagan life of sinful indulgence. But neither is it to be had from the law, any external law, even the Mosaic law. It is to be had only in Christ and in his Spirit who now becomes the only law, an internal law, by which the Christian lives. The purpose of the law is to reveal to man that he fails, that he needs salvation. The Christian presumably has faced that failure and, in Christ's risen life, overcome it. He is a changed man. What if he should fail again? Then, of course, he again needs the law. Serious sin in the Christian is treated by the

New Testament as tantamount to apostasy. The remedy is the sacrament of penance which the early Fathers did not hesitate to call a second baptism, thus making it a new death to sin and a new resurrection to the freedom of the inner norm of morality in the Spirit. Biblical morality, then, is not a sin-oriented morality but a morality based on the fact that we are sons with the Son in the freedom of his Spirit.

Can biblical morality be more specific? Does it provide any divinely inspired directives to help the Christian respond freely to the inner norm of the Spirit? Can these be organized in any systematic way? One principle for practical behavior can be found in the biblical doctrine that man is created in the image of God. This would lead the man responding in faith to God to want to perfect that image and to make it more operative in his life. Refusal to be an image of God is a refusal of faith to God, and it can be called sin. Even the Mosaic law, including the Ten Commandments, was less a matter of "natural law" or ritualistic fetish than it was a conscious attempt on the part of Israel to be holy as their holy God and to revere, honor, and reflect that image in their holy lives and worship. The New Testament counterpart of this principle is the person of Christ who is himself the "image of the invisible God." Christ is personally God and so embodies for us everything that the divine life means and demands for men. The imitation of Christ is for the Christian the practical way to perfect in himself his creation in the image of God.

Even more specifically, the moral teaching of the Sacred Scripture gives prominence to certain characteristic ways of acting that we have come to call by the non-biblical name of virtues. Among these, love certainly holds a special place. Interestingly enough, however, the Scripture presents love more as an attribute of God than as a virtue for man. Love of God is rarely spoken of in Scripture apart from its counterpart of love of neighbor. What this seems to be telling us is that we are asked to imitate God's love for us, not so much by loving him directly in return, but rather by loving the neighbor. We thus return God's love through the neighbor, in the "sacrament of the neighbor," as some contemporary theologians would say. Love, so understood, thus contributes directly to the building up of the social salvation community.

Faith is the characteristic response that Scripture emphasizes as demanded of man. In the biblical sense, faith means a total openness to God, a willingness to trust God and the working of his plan, an acceptance of the truth of God's word, a hope for its fulfillment and realization. Thus biblical faith has a much wider connotation than is usually given to this "virtue" in standard treatises. In this sense, faith includes hope and love of God. It flows over into the love of neighbor, active witness, and active apostolic zeal. Biblical faith should be as strong as Abraham's, as trusting as Peter's: "Lord, to whom shall we go? Thou hast the words of eternal life" (Jn 6:69).

Justice in the Bible is something very different from what we understand by human justice. Justice, like love, is more an attribute of God than a virtue in man. Justice is rooted in God's fidelity to his promises, his loving will to effect his plan of salvation. It is by God's justice that Christ brings our salvation. As a moral ideal for man, then, the biblical notion of justice is mostly related to zeal for the growth of the salvation kingdom. Prudence undergoes a similar transformation. The emphasis in prudence is less on a "golden mean" or "freedom from excess" than on seizing the right moment, "reading the signs of the times" as they relate to salvation history. Human wisdom, too, is to be modeled on divine wisdom, and the same is true of forgiveness. All of these moral qualities, in short, are but specifications of ways in which man is called to be truly an image of God in imitation of Christ and in response to the life of the Spirit within him.

Biblical morality, then, has much to contribute to a reform of the teaching and scientific structure of moral theology. It has great practical implications, too, for the pastoral work of preaching and catechetics. A morality firmly rooted in the Bible will hardly want to emphasize the narrow juridicism, the external conformity, and the complicated casuistry that have for so long characterized this field. Neither will moral science derive solely from a priori Greek abstractions about the nature of man and human perfectibility. Rather it will stress personal engagement in dialogue, faith-response to the initiative of God's love, love of neighbor in imitation of God's love and for the building up of the salvation community, freedom from slavery both to sin and to the law, the full freedom of total response to the dignity of sonship with Christ in the dynamic life of the Spirit. It is the editor's hope that the essays that follow will help more fully to illuminate these points. In that way a corrective can be applied to less biblical approaches presently in vogue and a stimulus supplied for a fully developed biblical morality yet to come.

I. COMMANDMENT

The Word of God

When all these things which I have set before you, the blessings and curses are fulfilled in you, and from among whatever nations the Lord, your God, may have dispersed you, you ponder them in your heart: then, provided that you and your children return to the Lord, your God, and heed his voice with all your heart and all your soul, just as I now command you, the Lord, your God, will change your lot; and taking pity on you, he will again gather you from all the nations wherein he has scattered you. Though you may have been driven to the farthest corner of the world, even from there will he bring you back. The Lord, your God, will then bring you into the land which your fathers once occupied, that you too may occupy it, and he will make you more prosperous and numerous than your fathers. The Lord, your God, will circumcise your hearts and the hearts of your descendants, that you may love the Lord, your God, with all your heart and all your soul, and so may live. But all those curses the Lord, your God, will assign to your enemies and the foes who persecuted you. You, however, must again heed the Lord's voice and carry out all his commandments which I now enjoin on you. Then the Lord, your God, will increase in more than goodly measure the returns from all your labors, the fruit of your womb, the offspring of your livestock, and the produce of your soil; for the Lord, your God, will take delight in your prosperity, even as he took delight in your fathers', if only you heed the voice of the Lord, your God, and keep his commandments and statutes that are written in this Book of the Law, when you return to the Lord, your God, with all your heart and all your soul.

7

For this command which I enjoin on you today is not too mysterious and remote for you. It is not up in the sky, that you should say, "Who will go up in the sky to get it for us and tell us of it, that we may carry it out?" Nor is it across the sea, that you should say, "Who will cross the sea to get it for us and tell us of it, that we may carry it out?" No, it is something very near to, already in your mouths and in your hearts; you have only to carry it out.

Here, then, I have today set before you life and prosperity, death and doom. If you obey the commandments of the Lord, your God, which I enjoin on you today, loving him, and walking in his ways, and keeping his commandments, statutes and decrees, you will live and grow numerous, and the Lord, your God, will bless you in the land you are entering to occupy. If, however, you turn away your hearts and will not listen, but are led astray and adore and serve other gods, I tell you now that you will certainly perish; you will not have a long life on the land which you are crossing the Jordan to enter and occupy. I call heaven and earth today to witness against you: I have set before you life and death, the blessing and the curse. Choose life, then, that you and your descendants may live, by loving the Lord, your God, heeding his voice, and holding fast to him. For that will mean life for you, a long life for you to live on the land which the Lord swore he would give to your fathers Abraham, Isaac and Jacob.

(Deuteronomy 30:1–20)

MATTHEW J. O'CONNELL, S.J.

Some Aspects of Commandment in the Old Testament

The assiduous reader will discover in these excerpts from a longer essay a discussion of questions such as these: What is the connection between the law of the Old Testament and the God of the covenant? How does the formulation of the law reflect its divine source? Did Israel look upon the Decalogue as a formulation of natural law? What is the purpose of the divine election of Israel? How is Israel's holiness related to covenant election? How is election related to commandment? What was Israel's "bill of rights"? What are the negative and positive aspects of Israel's holiness? How does love become an object of the commandment? If love is free how can it be commanded? How is the imperative of love related to God's redemptive purpose? Does the law, so understood, have any relation to the Gospel? How does Deuteronomy relate obedience to material prosperity? To life itself? What is the difference between Deuteronomy and Psalm 119 (Catholic version, 118) in its understanding of life? What does this difference imply relative to observance of the commandment? How does Deuteronomy express the existential and urgent character of the commandment? How does a proper understanding of commandment deepen our sense of personal relationship to God?

Father Matthew O'Connell is professor of theology at Woodstock College and Fordham University.

Commandment (*Entolē*) and Covenant

The most fundamental fact about law throughout the Old Testament is that it issues from the God of the covenant ("God of

These excerpts are reprinted with permission from an article entitled "Commandment in the Old Testament," *Theological Studies*, 21, 3 (September 1960).

Israel") and can be properly understood only in the framework of covenant and ultimately of election.[1] When the laws claim to be of divine origin (explicitly, e.g., at the beginning of the Decalogue, Ex 20:2, in the formulas of the holiness code, and in the apodictic laws in general; implicitly, e.g., in the structure of Dt,[2] where Moses speaks as prophet, as mediator between God and the people), this is not a transcendental claim based on an essential and timeless relation of human nature to God (as in the unwritten laws of Zeus in the *Antigone,* and in the Western tradition of natural law). It is an historical claim: the law is the will of the God of the covenant.

This connection between the law and the events of the desert and Sinai is clearly and constantly stated. There is, e.g., the introduction to the Decalogue (Ex 20:2): "I am the Lord your God, who led you out of the land of Egypt, out of the house of bondage." In Leviticus there is the frequent reminder of this same liberation and of the Egyptian past (Lv 18:3; 19:34, 36; 22:32f.; 25:38, 42, 55; 26:13, 45); the recurring "I am Yahweh" has the same significance. In Dt, besides the lengthier expositions in the discourses (cf., e.g., 4:32–38), there is the frequent grounding of particular laws with a reminder of the Egyptian slavery and Yahweh's liberation. These reminders are not only an incentive to humane conduct towards others; they also call to mind the source of the law and of its obligation (Dt 13:6, 11; 15:15; 20:1; 23:5; 24:9, 18; 25:17). It is unnecessary to cite chapter and verse to prove that the connection between covenant and Israelite law is verified in particular, and especially, of *entolē* (commandment).[3] Dt not only gives pre-eminence to *entolē* but is particularly concerned to relate Israel's life under law to the enduring covenant.

Up to this point we have simply the fact of a relationship between *entolē* and covenant. How are we to conceive of this relationship? Is it enough to say that God showed his favor to Israel and promised it land, "life," and posterity, and that Israel, in return, is to obey all his laws? In other words, that law and covenant are related only extrinsically, in that both have God for their source? This view contains an inadequate appreciation of the significance of the law, and indeed is misleading. It implies that the law is, for Israel, simply a perduring test of fidelity and, for all that Israel might know, quite arbitrary. To avoid this last conclusion, one appeals to the natural-law character of the Decalogue, the fundamental law of Israel. But this, we have seen, is not the Israelite viewpoint on the foundation of their law. If the Old Testament outlook on law and on life as lived in the framework of the law is not to be caricatured, we must penetrate more deeply into the relationship between covenant and law. The key to this relationship lies in a third concept, that of election. It is this that gives the covenant and ultimately the law their context and significance.

According to the picture presented to us in Dt, God first chose the patriarchs, with whom he then made a covenant (Dt 4:31) and to whom he gave promises (Dt 1:8; 6:10, etc.), and later he chose Israel. It was out of fidelity to his covenant with, and his promises to, the fathers that he chose Israel. This fidelity assures the permanence of the election; associated with this fidelity and even antecedent to it (as the ground of his free choice) is the goodness (*ḥesed*) of God, which assures that he will do more than simply carry out his part in the relationship of election: he will pardon Israel when it fails to do its part. The election is, then, the initial act by which Yahweh enters into relationship with his people, and the permanent reality which guarantees the continuance of the bond.

What, precisely, is the meaning of election? Vriezen, in his recent study, explains that the general sense of the word "elect" (*bāḥar. erwählen*), present in all its uses, is: to determine or dispose of something. The motives, of course, by which one is governed in actually making use of the person or thing one has at one's disposal, may differ widely. In the religious vocabulary of the Old Testament, however, the stress is placed on God's love as the motive of election; Israel has no inherent value which could motivate God's action (cf. Dt 7:7–8; 9:24). A second idea which attaches to the verb "elect" in its concrete use is that of commissioning, of appointing to a task. Election is always purposeful; one is elected in order to achieve a definite goal. Election also implies, indeed, a separation, but separation is only the negative side of election and is subordinate to the aspect of purpose. Vriezen sums up thus: "Election, in the full sense of the word, is a word with a nucleus (*Kern*) and two quite distinct subordinate ideas (*Nebengedanken*): one who is elected is thus one whom God, with a definite motive, removes from a crowd and commissions with a determinate task." [4]

What is the purpose of the divine election of Israel, according to Dt? "You are a people consecrated to the Lord your God, and the Lord your God has chosen you to be his very own people from among all the nations on the face of the earth" (7:6). "The Lord has taken you today to be his very own people . . . to be a people consecrated to the Lord your God." [5] Israel's destiny, then, is to be a holy people, that is, a people consecrated to God, belonging to him as a people peculiarly his own. Because of this destiny, the covenant, in which the election is concretized, is not a static relationship but rather the genetic principle of Israel's history, that is, of Israel's effort—made, indeed, in no unswerving or unflagging or unambiguous fashion—to co-operate with God in the realization of his purposes. "Co-operate with God": for in the covenant Israel's active role, though not on a plane with that of God,[6] is nonetheless completely necessary in order to establish that relationship of mutual belonging which sums up the covenant and constitutes (for Dt) Israel's task within the covenant: "Today you have taken God for your God . . . and the Lord has taken you today for His own people" (Dt 26:17-18).

It is true, of course, that by God's election and covenant Israel already *is* a consecrated people, God's special possession; such a status could only, indeed, be his free gift, it could only be a status conferred by God, not one achieved by purely human effort. From this point of view the law is a *sign* of Israel's consecration and special relationship to God, and obedience a *response* to an already existing relationship.[7] But this consecration does not imply any holiness inherent in Israel; Dt is quite clear on this; compare, e.g., 9:4ff.; 5:29. The holiness given Israel in the election and covenant is precisely that of a vocation.[8] Israel's holiness is thus not only a gift but also, and primarily, a project; "holy people" states not only a fact but a program. Israel must become what it is.

It is in this light that the *entolai* (the personal will of the covenant God) and especially the *entolē* (of 30:11-14), which is the unity of all the *entolai* and thus the center and summation of Dt, assume their full meaning. The Deuteronomic *entolē* is the creative and redemptive pattern, revealed by God, for Israel's existence as his holy people. Here the unity which we have seen the Deuteronomic *entolē* to possess (a unity of origin in the divine will and a unity of structure) acquires a new dimension: a unity of end and purpose.

To describe the *entolē* in this fashion is to say that Israel's national security, prosperity, and possession of the land were not the primary purpose of the law, but that holiness was. God's election had, indeed, meant "political" freedom for the seminomadic tribes that came out of Egypt, and this liberation was deeply, ineradicably impressed upon Israel's historical memory. God had rescued them from servitude to men, and from the disaggregation and chaos of their life in Egypt; the law, by ordering their life, gave them justice and security, and by pre-empting their service for God, put a seal upon their freedom. The Decalogue was their "bill of rights"; on this level, the law was a continuation of their liberation from Egypt and creative of "life," both in the sense that justice and security were a natural product of obedience to law and in the sense that God attached material prosperity to obedience.[9] On the other hand, Israel's "bill of rights" was also, and primarily, their obligations to God in the covenant.[10] And Israel was often to become conscious, in the course of her history, that her religious obligations and her national aims were not in tensionless harmony.[11] As for Dt, the destruction of the nation is clearly envisaged as a real possibility; God's will and purposes are, therefore, primary, and it is by her attitude to these that Israel stands or falls.

It follows from this that the strong stress laid in Dt on prosperity and "long life in the land" does not mean that these goods are the primary aim of the law. Dt is addressed to a nation whose recent history was "six centuries wasted in sin and constant apostasy"; [12] compare Dt *passim*. This people had only to be exhorted to love and fear God and to make of themselves a holy people; they had also to be enticed by the prospect of material well-being.[13] It was only through complete and inward obedience that they could gradually come to understand the purposes of God and enter into them (cf. Dt 29:2-9).

The primary significance of the Deuteronomic *entolē* is, then, that it is a pattern of life intended to make of Israel a holy people.[14] This can be shown in a positive manner in Dt; we cannot, however, expect to find it stated in so many words, for Dt is not a theological tract but an exhortation aiming at action and concentrating, therefore, on proposing those motives that will stir men to action.

To be "holy" means, negatively, to be separated, free, from all evil and defilement. This is precisely the effect which Dt intends certain of the laws to have. This is particularly true of laws against idolatry; see especially 4:15-20, where the prohibition is set in direct relation with the purpose of Israel's election: "Yahweh has brought you out of the iron furnace, Egypt, that you might become the people of his inheritance" (*Bible de Jérusalem*). The same aim of removing evil from the midst is attributed to other laws as well: e.g., murder (19:13) and false witness (19:19).

The more important positive side of Israel's holiness is given varied expression. We may distinguish two major facets of this holiness. The first is the communion with God to be achieved through mutual love: "That man's vocation is to love God is the secret revealed by the covenant to all who adhere to it." [15] The second element is that of *Nachfolge,* of following after God. This latter aspect of Israel's holiness will engage our attention later on—from a different viewpoint, but nonetheless completing, clearly enough, what is said in this section. It may seem that we have omitted from our consideration of "holiness" in Dt an important third aspect, that of the Israelite's *ḥesed* towards his fellow men in the covenant. Actually it has not been omitted; in Dt fraternal love [16] is presented as a reflection on the human level of God's love and *ḥesed* towards Israel, and it is under the rubric of *Nachfolge* that we envisage it. For the moment, then, let us return to love as part of Israel's holiness, and ask what it means that love should be the object or content of *entolē* and what this signifies for our understanding of *entolē.*

That love for God should be the object of *entolē* seems to many to be impossible; they see in the command to love "a juridical caricature of love for God, which cannot be extorted from man by a legal imperative." [17] This objection can be a legitimate one. Often it is not, namely, when love is thought of in primarily emotional terms. It is indeed true that "to love" (*'āhēb–agapein*) has in Dt a strong affective note, which is emphasized in the use of "to cleave to" (*dābaq*— e.g., *proskollasthai*) as a synonym. But the close link between love and observance of the commandments shows that Dt puts primary stress on the voluntary character of this love. However, even if we set aside, as being secondary, the emotional aspects of love for God, nonetheless as long as we distinguish love, as an interior attitude of active self-surrender, both from the outward manifestations of love itself and from other interior attitudes, such as reverential fear, the problem in some sort remains: how can such an attitude be commanded?

Two aspects of love must be reconciled. It is free (certainly when it has God for its object) and therefore can be required of man by God. On the other hand, love is a mode of existing, a function of man's total life, not an isolated, rootless will-act. If love, then, is "commanded," it cannot be commanded the way, for example, that an exterior act can be required. Fundamental inner attitudes, such as love, are essentially responses to values which make themselves

known to man in one or another fashion. It is true that the presence
and strength and genuineness of these responses can be tested by
the criterion of works and specifically, in the case of love for God, of
"keeping the commandments." It is true, in addition, that such responses can be objectified and grouped with exterior actions, even
with the most superficial *actus humani,* under the common rubric
of moral action. But they are in themselves not identical with such
exterior actions. Being vital, though free, responses, they depend, if
they are authentic, on a man's whole outlook; they express, each in
its own way (love, reverence, fidelity, truthfulness), the orientation
of his personality.

All this is obvious enough. It is mentioned here only as a background against which to appreciate the thought of Dt. The Deuteronomist presents the great fundamental attitudes of love and reverential fear as the response which man owes to the saving love
and power of God the Lord (cf. chap. 6 as a whole).[18] Love is indeed "commanded" ("Thou shalt"), but it is not commanded in the
same sense that the avoidance of idolatry, e.g., is commanded. The
prohibition against idolatry can be given specific legal forms (speci-
fying which acts are idolatrous, etc.) and sanctions. Love as such
cannot, but only the works which proceed, or ought to proceed,
from love.

Again, Dt "commands" the love of God, but it does not intend to
awaken love by commanding it. Love is awakened by the experience
of being loved, and Dt dwells, for this reason, on the intensity and
generosity of God's love for Israel. The purpose of the "command"
is to recall man to his responsibility and to rouse him to the need of
removing the obstacles within himself which stand in the way of his
proper response to God. But the response itself flows from insight
into the great love and goodness of God for Israel.[19]

These considerations show that love can be "commanded" without
its unique character being betrayed—provided that we do not understand "commandment" in too narrowly legalistic a fashion. Nonetheless, given the influence which words exert upon our concepts, it
would certainly be better if we could find a term which does not
have the juridical connotations of "command." Even the somewhat
awkward "imperative of love" seems preferable and we shall use it
from now on.

We may now ask whether this discussion of the imperative of love
and of its meaning in Dt has advanced our understanding of the

Deuteronomic *entolē*. It seems that it has. The pattern of life which
the *entolē* reveals to Israel is already a great gift, by the mere fact
that it insures the abiding presence of God among his people (4:7)
and a manner of life built upon just foundations (4:8). Now, however, with the inclusion of the imperative of love, the *entolē* becomes
an even more precious gift. For it reveals that the fundamental
theme in God's relation to man is his permanent desire for intimate
communion with man, and thereby it removes, in the most radical
manner possible, all fear on man's part of arbitrary rejection by God.
This new revelation increases, of course, the seriousness of the Israelite's vocation: he now understands that the will of God can be
fully carried out only if obedience is the expression of a love uniting
him to God who has loved him first. At the same time, however, the
imperative of love prevents the Israelite's existence from degenerat-
ing into a crushing and chaotic multiplicity of lifeless external actions, and thus it simplifies his situation before God.

What is more important: in the imperative of love, law is carried
into the heart to become a transforming force. The Deuteronomic
entolē is, in the divine intention, "redemptive." This word, as applied to law, may seem unjustified. But if properly understood, it
can be legitimately used. The sense is not that law itself could effect
any kind of holiness; no norm of action can, not even the "new
entolē" of St. John. And Israel's history was to show well enough that
the law alone, however perfect, was not enough of a stimulus to
overcome man's hardness of heart. For that to happen, the law of
love had to become the law of the Spirit.

The sense of "redemptive," then, as applied to law is simply that
in the divine intention the law is a prolongation of God's saving
action in the Exodus and a means of realizing his redemptive purpose in Israel and ultimately, through Israel, in the whole world.[20]
Here, of course, we must think of God's "salvation" at the Exodus
as being more than something of the natural or political order. Redemption "from" something appears usually, it is true, only in the
generic reference to the liberation from enslavement in Egypt. But
something of a higher order is everywhere implicit. Consider, for
example, Numbers 15:39–41, which concerns the Israelite's wearing
a hem on his garments to remind him of the law. Here it is said that
the purpose of the *entolai* and the effect of obedience will be the
sundering of man's solidarity with his own evil desires, which lead
him from God, and with all outside of himself that is profane, and
communion, instead, with God who liberated him from Egypt that

He might become his God. Dt's insistence on laws against idolatry may be read as a similar commentary on the redemptive character of the law; for Dt here merely reflects Israel's past history: her natural tendency, always breaking out anew, to fall back into subjection to false gods and to the corruption that went with their worship.

To appreciate properly, therefore, the Old Testament attitude towards the law, it has to be read, not in the light of St. Paul's statement: "It [the Law] was enacted on account of transgressions [i.e., to provoke them]," [21] but in the light of his other statement: "the Law indeed is holy and the commandment holy and just and good" (Rom 7:12). The law could not indeed achieve its own purpose, and therefore it is linked with judgment. But it is not on this account to be opposed radically to "gospel," i.e., to grace and promise. Law for the Old Testament, and for Dt in particular, is a part, or a prolongation, of gospel. So much so that the "law" of the New Testament is, from one point of view at least, a fulfilling and perfecting of the old law.[22]

Our findings may be summarized as follows. Law, for the Old Testament, directly expresses the will of the God of the covenant. This does not mean, however, that law is to be regarded purely as a condition, arbitrary in its stipulations, of God's fulfillment of his promises. There is an inner necessity in the law. But it is grounded, not a priori in the demands of a humanitarian ideal nor in a determination of what human nature requires for its perfection, but in Israel's vocation and in the purpose to which the acceptance of that vocation, in the covenant, committed it. Israel's vocation was to be a holy people, a people belonging entirely to God. In this light the Deuteronomic *entolē* (cf. 30:11–14) may be defined or described as the creative and redemptive pattern, revealed by God, for Israel's existence as his holy people. This holiness demanded, negatively, a separation of Israel from all evil and, on the positive side, a communion with God in mutual love, a "following after Yahweh," and a certain kind of "life." We have touched briefly upon the first of these positive aspects, insofar as the problem arises of how love can be the object of *entolē*, of a "command."

"The Commandments of Life" (Baruch 3:9)

One of the characteristic marks of Old Testament thought is the connecting of "life" with the will of God as expressed in the law. That "life" should be associated with *entolē* is, then, to be expected.

Nevertheless, since this association provides one of the major contexts of *entolē*, both *entolē* and "life" being so central to Dt, it deserves some notice if our study is to touch on the major themes connected with the *entolē*.

"Life" in the Old Testament is far too large and complicated a subject to venture into here for its own sake. Instead, let us ask simply: What does "life" mean as an effect of the *entolē*, first in Dt and then in our second major source on *entolē*, viz., Psalm 119?

In Dt the result of obedience to the will of God in the law is expressed in several ways: "that it may be well with you" (4:40; 5:16; 6:3, 18; etc.); "that you may prolong your days in the land which the Lord gives you" (4:40; 5:16, 33; 11:9; etc.); "that the Lord may bless you" (14:29; 23:20; cf. 1:11; 7:13; 15:8, etc.). In many of the phrases about the land Dt insists that it is an "inheritance" (4:21, 38; 12:9; 15:4; etc.). A further modality of the possession of the land is that this possession is a "rest" after the wilderness marches and the conquest (3:20; 12:9, 10; 25:19). The primarily material character of the prosperity which obedience will bring to Israel emerges quite unequivocally in the list of blessings in chapter 28.

Dt does not reflect on the precise relationship that exists between obedience and these manifold material results. It does not raise the objection which the Israelite knew as well as any one else: that the just do not always prosper and the wicked often do. However, it can be argued that for Dt, from its particular viewpoint, the objection is not valid. Dt addresses the people as a whole, precisely as a people, and it is convinced that if the whole people were to be loyal to God and to become truly a holy people, all this prosperity would come to pass, God's promises would be fulfilled. Even the individual, for whom the promise of "length of days" seems necessarily intended, will enjoy this blessing only if the whole people is loyal, just as, in turn, his individual sin is an infection that must be purged out lest the whole community suffer (cf. Dt 13:5; 17:7; 19:10; 21:23; 24:6).

The state of prosperity which Israel's complete loyalty would inaugurate is a state of affairs that can be realized in this life, on this earth. For the Deuteronomist, there can be no objection on the grounds of the laws of nature. Nature is entirely subject to God and placed by him in the service of his alliance with Israel.[23] It may be said, then, that the relation between obedience and material prosperity is not a problem for Dt: if Israel is loyal, God will keep his promises. This view of the link between prosperity and obedience is not extreme naïveté nor is it the unscrupulous rhetoric of one enamored of law and determined to win acceptance of it. The prophets share the same view, even in noneschatological passages. Compare Isaia 48:18: "If you had only been attentive to my commandments! Like a river would have been your prosperity and your righteousness like the waves of the sea." [24]

Is the Deuteronomic view of "life"—it must be kept in mind that we are speaking of "life" in the couple "commandments and life"—limited to a "long and happy life in the land of inheritance"? Some texts seem to suggest that something of a higher order is meant. In Dt 32:47 we read: "for this [the law] is by no means too trivial a thing for you to do; on the contrary it means your life"; and in 8:3: "to show you that man does not live only by bread but that man lives by everything that comes forth from the mouth of God." There is danger, however, of reading into these texts ideas which are actually strange to them. It would be difficult to show that in 32:47 we have anything more than a variation on 30:15, 19, where the Israelite hears the law read to him and is placed before a decision of life or death. In this latter text the "life" is that of which Dt continually speaks: the life of the people in the Promised Land, and the "death" is that sketched graphically in the curses of 28:15–68 and in the exile prediction of 4:25–39. The context of the words cited from Dt 32:47 makes it especially difficult to read into "life" anything more than we find elsewhere; for the text continues: "(it means your life) and for this very reason you shall live long in the land into which you are crossing the Jordan for conquest." Do not "life" and "live" here refer to the same reality?

In Dt 8:3 it is tempting to see two kinds of life referred to, but does the text actually mean more than that the life of the Israelite—his material life and prosperity—depends not only on having bread to eat but on obedience to the word of God? But however this text be taken, it is safe to say that there is very little evidence in Dt for seeing in the term "life" anything of a different order than what we have already referred to. This, of course, does *not* mean that Dt does not know of a higher life than the material! All that has been said of the Israelite's vocation to love God and to imitate him shows this. But our question here has been only: What is the significance of the term "life" in the couple, commandments and life?

When we turn to Psalm 119, we are in a quite different atmosphere. The Psalm is an expression of individual piety, although it may be assumed to be representative of what other men of the time felt.[25] The composers of Psalms 1 and 19 must have had rather much the same attitude to the law as the composer of 119; as must, too, the man who prays in Psalm 40:9: "To do thy will, my God, is my pleasure, and I carry your law in my heart" (Weiser), or the man who is described in Psalm 37:31. What, then, is the link between law and "life" in Psalm 119?

"In them [your ordinances] you gave me life" (Ps 119:93). Here we have a sentence very similar to that of Leviticus 18:5: "In them you shall live." Is the sense the same? Undoubtedly, the "life" which the Psalmist has received in time of danger (v. 92) or prays for in similar circumstances (vv. 17, 18, 117, 174) is a continued physical existence upon earth. Yet these very petitions show that "life" has a higher meaning as well: "In accordance with thy kindness (*hesed*) revive me, that I may observe the decrees of thy mouth" (v. 88). This continued physical existence is also a life whose structure and significance are determined by obedience to the will of God. The *tôrâ* is *the* great gift of God (v. 29), and the petitions of verse 144 ("Thy decrees are eternally right [*s^{e}dāqâ*]. Give me understanding that I may live!") and of verse 10 ("I seek thee with my whole heart; let me not wander from thy *entolai!*") show clearly that for the Psalmist " 'to have life' means . . . not only earthly existence but also that higher interior life of moral union with God who encounters man in the law, which alone makes life truly worth living to the writer." [26] To return to verse 93, we can say that in Psalm 119 "life" means not only continuing physical existence, which, in the experience of the Psalmist, itself comes to him due to his obedience to the divine will (v. 92, etc.), but an interior life consisting in the knowledge and fulfillment of that will.

Upon this foundation, derived from the verses which speak explicitly of law and life, we can construct a fuller picture of what life means for the Psalmist, that inner life which flows from the fulfillment of the divine will or, more accurately, which *is* the fulfillment of the divine will: a life according to the divine will is its own reward (v. 112). This is not a colorless life, the gray existence of the letter-bound Pharisee. For the Psalmist, the commandments of God are the source of delight and deepest joy (vv. 16, 143); the laws of God have become for him "songs . . . in the house of my pilgrimage" (v. 54), his light (v. 105), honey in his mouth (v. 103), and water for his parched spirit (v. 131), a treasure more precious than any earthly riches (vv. 14, 72, 127).

The *tôrâ* (and *tôrâ* means for Psalm 119, as was noted above, the whole of divine revelation; it corresponds to the *entolē* of Dt) is a great and marvelous world of its own (vv. 18, 129), and in it the Psalmist finds freedom of soul, an enlargement and flowering of his spirit. The word used in verse 45 and translated in English as "at large" is an adjective used substantively. In this form it does not appear elsewhere in the Psalter but is used to describe the Promised Land in Exodus 3:8. Given this identification, or implication of identity, of the *tôrâ* and the Promised Land, it is not surprising to find the Psalmist adopting the great Deuteronomic word "inheritance" and applying it to the tôrâ: "Your testimonies are my inheritance forever, they are the joy of my heart" (v. 111, *Bible de Jérusalem*). "Instead of the Promised Land the revelation of Yahweh's will has become his true *nahalah* and the pledge of covenant loyalty. For him the fulfillment of the commandments is no longer primarily the condition for securing earthly blessing nor even . . . the gifts of salvation; it is the divine instruction that, as such, becomes the essential covenant gift." [27] Thus, with the interiorization of the concept of life and the identification of true life with the joyful, liberating fulfillment of the divine will, the vocabulary associated throughout Israelite history with the Promised Land has also been interiorized.

Two further Deuteronomic themes have been called upon and submitted to this same process of interiorization. The wisdom, which in Dt 4:6 was attributed to Israel because they possessed so good a law, now becomes a wisdom flowing from the fulfillment of the law (vv. 98–100, 104, 130). In Dt 4:7 the law had been the sign of God's salvific presence among his people; in Psalm 119:151 the commandments, with their "truth" ('*emet*), are the locus and medium of God's salvific presence in the soul of the Psalmist: "Thou art near, O Lord, and all thy commandments are truth."

In this transformation of Deuteronomic themes it can be said that Dt has been carried to its logical conclusion and at the same time fulfilled. It has been carried to its logical conclusion: in Dt the law itself had been interiorized, when the root of all obedience was placed in the heart with the imperative of love, and obedience was made a matter of the imitation of God. The law was thus in its whole tendency a medium of communion between God and man.

At the same time, however, the reward of obedience, the "life" which the law purported to help man achieve, had been limited to physical life and material well-being. Such life and prosperity, whenever approximated in Israel's history, had proved rather an incentive to "forget Yahweh" than a stimulus of gratitude; and the prophets had to preach that such prosperity was safe only in the eschatological period when all "Israel"—the spiritual Israel—would have turned to God. During the present life, God alone must be the goal of man's striving. In applying to God himself and to his will the Deuteronomic "inheritance" and the vocabulary of the Promised Land, and in attaching to God and his will the power of emotional attraction which such words as "inheritance" exerted upon the Israelite soul, Psalm 119 was carrying out the real intention of Dt, which was to lead Israel to "love the Lord your God with all your mind and all your heart and all your strength." At the same time Dt has been fulfilled: the Deuteronomic *entolē*—the *tôrâ* of Psalm 119—has proved to be for the Psalmist a truly "creative and redemptive pattern of life."

The Existential Quality of the Legal *Entolē*

The adjective "existential," as applied to the divine *entolē* in the law, might signify that the divine will lays claim upon the whole of man's life, in its least details as well as in its broad outlines; that the creative and liberating form and pattern which the *entolē* reveals absorbs human activity in all its ramifications. Here, however, we use "existential" rather to characterize the "here and now" quality which attaches to the *entolē*. This aspect of the *entolē* finds its expression, in Dt, in the "today" which is a leitmotiv of this book and gives a particular coloring to its major themes of election, covenant, and *entolē*.

Dt is presented as a speech of Moses to the people, and the "today" is, in the first instance, the day on which he expounds the Deuteronomic *tôrâ*. Dt is, on the other hand, not intended to be a purely historical record; it is also exhortation addressed to the "today" of its readers and hearers. "Hearers" is, indeed, the proper word; for "Deuteronomy in its present form is undoubtedly a literary production, but it still bears the stamp of a cultic form that has exercised an extraordinary influence on its style."[28] The cultic form in question is that of a feast of covenant renewal, for which Dt itself, in fact, makes provision (Dt 30:9–13). Thus the "today" on which Moses speaks becomes the "today" of each cultic renewal of the covenant.[29]

This cultic renewal is not to be imagined simply as a reading of Dt, much as we read the Gospel in the church today. For the Israelite, as for the peoples of the ancient Near East generally, cult took the form of dramatic presentation, so that the Deuteronomic "today" can be called the "today" of "cultic actualization."

It is important not to misunderstand the nature of the "actualization," of "making present" the historical events of Sinai. The cultic drama was more than a stage play (as we might stage a play portraying the signing of the Declaration of Independence), but it was also something quite other than a renewal effected magically by virtue of the sacred words and actions themselves, such as is found in renewal rites of the ancient Near East outside of Israel. The cult was the locus of the renewal of the covenant, but the renewal was effected in faith, by a meeting of two wills: God offering his covenant and man accepting it. The offering of the covenant to Israel was a timeless action, not in the sense that myth is timeless (myth does not record a historic fact but mirrors the destiny of man; of any myth it can be said: "This never happened, but always is"[30]), but in the sense that God's action was intended to affect, was valid for, every generation. The events of Sinai were "today" for each generation in Israel and for each individual Israelite, because God was equally present to each.

"Today," then, ever anew God chooses Israel (Dt 5:3), and Israel becomes the people of God (27:9); "today" Israel crosses the Jordan (9:1) and is given the Promised Land (9:3). "Today" God reveals once again his will, the vital and liberating principle which will effectively make of Israel a holy people, God's possession and God's inheritance. And "today," finally, Israel must accept or reject this form and pattern of her life, knowing, as she makes her choice, that it is a decision between life and death.[31]

That this "today" of Dt is seriously and realistically meant, and not a simple rhetorical flourish, is clear from Dt 29:2–9: "Although you have seen all that the Lord did before your eyes in the land of Egypt to Pharaoh and all his courtiers and all his land, the great tests which you saw with your own eyes, the signs and those great portents, yet to this day the Lord has not given you a mind to understand, nor eyes to discern nor ears to hear. . . ."[32] Each

Israelite can say, and say each time that he hears or reads the Deuteronomic message, that he has not understood what God has done and that he has not fully shared in the great purpose of God: to make of Israel a holy people. To him, then, God's revelation is addressed as on the first day. Each moment of the Israelite's existence possesses, in relation to the will of God, a quality of uniqueness and vital decision.

From what we have said in the last three paragraphs, it is clear that the Deuteronomic stress on the contemporaneity of historical events does not volatilize history, destroy its character as *ephapax*, or turn it into myth. God both transcends history and is the God of *ḥesed* and *'emet* (cf. Dt 7:9). Therefore, the covenant, though made once, was made with every generation. The Israelite is not to act *as if* he were in the situation of Moses' followers; before God that *is* his situation.

In somewhat analogous fashion, the uniqueness of the decision before which the Deuteronomic *entolē* sets the Israelite at each moment of his existence does not destroy the abiding validity of the Decalogue. The Decalogue projects the structure of an existence in which the great motivating forces are the love and imitation of God. But since this structure is never fully achieved by the individual, it needs to be ever newly adopted as one's own and its purpose approved and accepted.

What, then, does the "today" tell us of the Deuteronomic *entolē*, in relation to the Israelite and in relation to God? For the Israelite it reveals the importance and decisiveness of each act of obedience to the *entolē*, each effort to make it his own vital life-form. The generation and the individual must share in the building up of the holy people through history. They cannot take refuge from their responsibility in a given and permanent order of things behind which God has, as it were, retreated, nor erect the law into a protective barrier between themselves and God. The *entolē*, in the light of the "today," is seen, from a new point of view, as a mode of the presence of God to man.[33]

The *entolē*, of course, in its fundamental content—the love and imitation of God in terms of the Decalogue—already guards against such an escape from personal commitment and responsibility. The "today" does not, then, introduce a properly new element into the *entolē*. It does bring out, however, the full significance and realism of the personal relationship which the *entolē*—when received into the heart and made the vital form and principle of existence— creates between man and God.

The *entolē* can also be regarded from the side of God, as something of and from him. From this point of view the "today" confirms what was said above in speaking of the vocabulary of "commandment," viz., that the contexts of *entellesthai* and *entolē* show that these terms stress the personal will of the God of the covenant and emphasize his authority present in his commandments. In addition, the "today" theme, by giving the legal *entolē*—even though the latter aims at creating a permanent structure of life—an aspect of the "ever new," brings out the dynamic and active character of the divine *entellesthai*.

What we have been saying in this section may seem a modern "existentialist" reading of Dt, a piece of eisegesis. It is instructive, therefore, to see the writer of Psalm 119 taking the attitude of a disciple in the presence of God who teaches him and speaks to him here and now through the pages of the Book (the *tôrâ* of Ps 119 is the written word of God: cf. the "anthological" construction of the whole Psalm). God spoke in the past, and this is recorded in the Book; yet he speaks now through the Book to the Psalmist. The latter's "fundamental concern is to confront man with God who speaks." [34] He turns especially to Dt. Passages like Dt 4:1-9 and 6:1-7, on which the Psalmist has fed his soul, are for him "not a dead legacy from the past, but a living testimony of the covenant grace, here and now bestowed upon him, of the life-giving God." [35] The Psalmist is doing, in the sphere of the individual, what Dt had already done for all Israel: given the past new significance and power for the present.

Conclusions on the Deuteronomic *Entolē* and *Entellesthai*

At the risk of excessive repetition let us sum up the conclusions we have come to, in the course of this essay, on *entolē*. The Deuteronomic *entolē* (the singular noun, taken in its special and inclusive Deuteronomic sense) is the constructive and liberating principle, form, and pattern whereby Israel is to fulfill its vocation as the holy people of God. The first and fundamental content of this *entolē* is the imperative of love (this is the vital and dynamic principle of Israel's mode of life). Love flowers into the pursuit of likeness to God (this pursuit gives the specific note or "form" of Israel's existence), which likeness is sketched out for Israel in the Decalogue (this last thus becomes the hard bony structure, the pattern, of Israelite existence).

The "following of Yahweh" (the pursuit of the divine likeness) gives to Israel's existence a quality of intimate communion with God (the effective realization of the communion which love already implies and strives for). It also means that, from God's side, the *entolē* is a revelation of himself.

The *entolē* is also a source of life, and in Psalm 119 this life is finally seen to be, not a reward exterior to the *entolē* ("life" in Dt as prosperous material existence), but as the *entolē* itself, accepted and becoming what it was intended to be, viz., a vital and liberating force, a medium of communion and a source of the "knowledge of God" which is one of the fundamental aspirations of the Old Testament (cf. Hos 2:22; Jer 31[38]:34).

The *entolē,* finally, as ever-new, as always of "today," becomes a mode of the presence of God to his people and an evidence of the dynamic and active quality of this presence.

From this study of *entolē* certain facets of *entellesthai* (as this verb is used in Dt and Ps 119, at least) come to light. Since *entolē* and *entellesthai* are but two aspects of the same thing, the object (*entolē*) giving us insight into the activity, we need merely apply what has been learned of *entolē*. Thus, the personal character of the divine *entellesthai* emerges clearly, as does its dynamic and active character.

Further, just as the *entolē* is the prolongation of God's grace and fidelity in the Exodus, so the *entellesthai*—the will of God establishing the law and bidding men obey it—is an activity of God's grace and fidelity. It is a "commanding" which is inspired by salvific love and which is, indeed, a function or aspect of the salvific will of God for Israel (and ultimately, through Israel, for the world: cf. Is 2:3). As it proceeds from love, so it aims at awaking a response of love, at creating a communion between God and men. It is the "commanding" of the unique and omnipotent Lord, but of a Lord who is also Father and Lover.

References

1 This statement, valid for the OT taken as a whole, does not mean that the association of law and covenant is equally strong in all strains of OT thought. Eichrodt (*Theologie des Altens Testaments,* III, 2nd ed. [Berlin, 1948], 77)

points out, e.g., how in the priestly tradition the divine will to sanctify man is closely linked with His creative will and thus tends to be independent of the existence of the "people" (which owes its origin to the covenant) and to become an absolute and universal will for man as such. M. Noth, *Die Gesetze im Pentateuch*, Parts 3 and 4, claims a much more complete dissociation of law and covenant in the postexilic period.

2 This abbreviation for "Deuteronomy" is used consistently throughout the text.—ED. NOTE

3 *Entolē* is used for "commandment" consistently throughout the text. This is the Greek noun used to translate Hebrew *miswâ*. In a previous section of the original article, the author has shown how *entolē* is used in Deuteronomy and the literature influenced by it to sum up the essence of the whole law and to feature its relation to Yahweh's sovereign will. Cf. the original article in *Theological Studies*, 21, 3 (September 1960), 351–403.—ED. NOTE

4 T. C. Vriezen, *Die Erwählung Israels nach dem Alten Testament* (Zurich, 1953), pp. 41–42.

5 Dt 26:18–19.

6 The covenant, like the election, is due solely to God's free initiative. Nor can it be said that once God made the covenant and Israel accepted it, his position of superiority in this relationship was in any way weakened. "Covenant," like any other term applied to God, can only be applied analogously. "This term was borrowed from the realm of law and given a special theological application. . . . In this case covenant is no longer a legal compact between human beings, but a device for explaining the meaning and nature of Israel's election" (Wright, *The Old Testament against Its Environment*, pp. 54–55). This kind of treaty or covenant between superior and inferior was not peculiar to Israel: cf. George E. Mendenhall, "Covenant Forms in Israelite Tradition," *Biblical Archaeologist*, 17 (1954), 50–76.

7 Cf. G. E. Wright, *Deuteronomy* (Interpreter's Bible, 2; New York–Nashville: Abingdon Press, 1953), p. 488 on Dt 26:6–19.

8 Cf. Vriezen, *op. cit.*, p. 57. André Neher, in his recent books on the prophets, has insisted strongly on the idea of a divine task given to man to be undertaken in cooperation with God, as being essential to a correct understanding of the Hebrew *berît* (*diathēkē*–covenant); cf., e.g., his *L'Essence du prophétisme* (Paris, 1955), pp. 117–18; his *Amos: Contribution à l'étude du prophétisme* (Paris, 1950), pp. 45–48 (on the covenant as a sharing of responsibilities) and pp. 242–44.

9 "Bill of rights": J. Coert Rylaarsdam, *Exodus* (Interpreter's Bible, 1), p. 843.

10 Cf. George E. Mendenhall, "Ancient Oriental and Biblical Law," *Biblical Archaeologist*, 17 (1954), 30; "Covenant Forms," *ibid.*, pp. 62–64.

11 Cf. Walther Eichrodt, *Man in the Old Testament* (Studies in Biblical Theology, 4; London, 1951), pp. 40–44, on Israel's religious development resulting from the opposition between her religious convictions and her national ambitions.

12 G. von Rad, *Studies in Deuteronomy* (London: Allenson, 1953), p. 70.

13 In any view this material well-being came from God, and von Rad is justified in saying that no materialistic spirit has crept into Dt.

14 The word "pattern" may be misleading. It does not mean a formula or a guide to be automatically followed (like a dressmaker's pattern) or a complete outline of what to do on each occasion. To present Israel with a "pattern" in any of these senses would be to favor concentration on outward observances, which Dt precisely does not do. By "pattern" here is meant simply that the

broad outlines of how the holy people is to live are revealed to Israel. There are, as will be pointed out in the text, two main points in this revelation: love as the fundamental motive or dynamic inner principle (this includes the reverence expressed in "fear") and the following of God's ways as the specifically Israelite "form" of life ("form" as giving the inner shape and peculiarly Israelite quality of religious life). The Decalogue is perhaps more justifiably called a "pattern," in a stricter use of the word, but it should be observed that the Decalogue is merely a sketch of God's "ways," a set of broad fundamental principles needing application. It is in terms of principles and applications that Dt conceives the relation between the Decalogue and the code, as is implied in Dt 5:22ff., where the people receive the Decalogue directly from God, but the "statutes and ordinances" indirectly through Moses (cf. Wright, *Deuteronomy*, on the passage). We shall henceforth freely use "pattern," "principle," "form," either of the *entolē* as a totality, or, as the context will indicate, of the commandment of love or the following of God in particular.

[15] Neher, *L'Essence du prophétisme*, p. 116.

[16] The commandment of fraternal love (Lv 19:18) does not appear in Dt, but "the omission . . . is only accidental, especially since the motive of brotherly love is so basic and prominent in the exposition of the law" (Wright, *Deuteronomy*, p. 401).

[17] The objection is thus formulated by Eichrodt, *Theologie*, I, 49. For an example of this outlook, cf. G. Quell on love in the OT (*TWNT*, 1, 20–34; translated into English by J. Coates, *Love* [Bible Key Words from Kittel's *TWNT*, 1; London, 1949]; cf. p. 7 of the English version).

[18] This statement can be applied to almost all of OT moral preaching: the Pentateuch, prophets, Psalms (though not the wisdom literature), but Dt stresses the "response" character of obedience more than other OT books. Cf., e.g., the long historical introduction (chaps. 1–3) and the conclusions drawn from this history in chap. 4. Notable also is the fact that the Sabbath commandment in Dt 5:15 is given a *heilsgeschichtlich* meaning, whereas Ex 20:11 grounds it in the "rest" of God after creation.

[19] Cf. Eichrodt, *Theologie*, III, 33.

[20] It is only with Second Isaia that Israel's mission to the whole of mankind comes to the fore (cf. Vriezen, *op. cit.*, pp. 64–72).

[21] Gal 3:19. On the interpretation given the text here, cf. S. Lyonnet, S.J., *Liberté chrétienne et loi de l'Esprit selon s. Paul* (reprinted from *Christus*, 4 [October 1954]), pp. 3–4; this interpretation, whether correct for St. Paul or not, serves to emphasize a contrast between two views of law and to situate the Deuteronomic view.

[22] Cf. Jn 1:16–17. The opposition between law and gospel, law and promise, depends very largely on the Pauline problematic of the law and thus, ultimately, on the Judaic idea of the law which Paul fought and in which the law had become self-sufficient. In older Israelite thought, on the contrary, law and promise or gospel are inseparable; the law, no less than the promises, is a gift, a grace, a proof of God's gracious mercy. This does not mean that while the initial response to the gift of promise-and-law is one of gratitude, it does not become further differentiated as a sense of responsibility toward the preceptive will of God. Undoubtedly, too, there came to the Israelite some of the same sense of insufficiency before the demands of the divine will which Paul expresses in Rom 7. Such a complex response is inevitable and is ultimately founded in what God and man are: God is both Lord and Savior, man both servant and saved. But it is an oversimplification to link God as Lord exclusively with law and God as Savior exclusively with the promises. For God may be said to be

most "Lord" when he is "Savior," and to become man's Savior, at least in part, in the very exercise of his Lordship in the law.

23 Cf. remarks of Wright, *Deuteronomy*, on 11:13–17 (p. 405) and on chap. 28 (pp. 493–94).

24 Translated from *Bible de Jérusalem;* cf. remarks of Eichrodt, *Man in the Old Testament*, p. 50.

25 In discussing Ps 119 we do not restrict ourselves to those verses which contain the word *entolē*. *Entolē* is in this Psalm one of a number of generally synonymous terms for divine revelation; these terms are, indeed, not always synonymously used and their extension differs considerably in many verses—a fact which must be respected, but in discussing the relation of law and life in the Psalm, there can be no objection in principle to making use of verses whose terms are synonymous with *entolē*. For Ps 119 as an expression of private piety, i.e., of its noncultic *Sitz im Leben*, cf. Deissler's discussion, *Psalm 119 [118] und seine Theologie* (Munich, 1955), pp. 281–87.

26 Deissler, *ibid.*, p. 240.

27 *Ibid.*, p. 210.

28 Von Rad, *Studies in Deuteronomy*, pp. 14–15.

29 The question of how often there actually was such a renewal, in pre-exilic times, is of course a difficult one; cf. Wright, *Deuteronomy*, pp. 512–13. But whether the cultic renewal occurred frequently or not does not affect our analysis of the significance of the "today," since the Israelite (and the Christian: cf. R. A. F. MacKenzie, S.J., "The Messianism of Deuteronomy," *CBQ*, 19 [1957], 299–305) who read Dt or heard it read, no less than the Israelite who assisted at the cultic renewal of the covenant, was invited to regard the "today" as addressed to himself.

30 Sallustius, apropos of the Atthis myth.

31 Dt 30:15–20. The alternatives set before the people, seen in sharpest form here (life or death) but occurring throughout Dt in one or other shape (cf. 7:12 and 8:19; 11:13, 16; 11:22; 26:16–19; 28), are one of the areas in which the Deuteronomist and the prophets think along similar lines.

32 Chaps. 28–29 do not seem to have been part of Dt in its first form; cf. Wright, *Deuteronomy*, p. 317, for a conservative view. In any case, these chapters do not change the thought of the previous chapters but simply stress the covenant idea which is fundamental to the whole of Dt.

33 It was said earlier that "in Ps 119:151, the commandments, with their 'truth' ('*emet*), are the locus and medium of God's salvific presence in the soul of the Psalmist." How does this differ from what has been said in the text above? In Ps 119 it is the existence of revelation which is the sign of God's presence, together with its attribute of '*emet*: the abiding and unchanging truth of the law, which gives the Psalmist certainty about what God's will is and, consequently, an assurance that his own existence, in following the law, is not an illusion (cf. Ps 119:6, 31, 80, 116). In a word, it is the law in its objective existence and content that is the medium and pledge of God's presence. From the viewpoint of the Deuteronomic "today," however, it is rather in the decision and responsibility before God—which the *entolē* forces upon man—that the presence of God is grasped: not in the objective content of the divine will, but in the "commanding" of it by God here and now, in the inescapable personal relationship. Ps 119, in fact, knows also this kind of divine presence, as the text above goes on to point out. But this aspect of the presence of God emerges from the whole ethos of the Psalm rather than from the explicit testimony of v. 151.

34 Deissler, *Psalm 119*, p. 269.

35 *Ibid.*, p. 271.

II. SIN

The Word of God

Have mercy on me, O God, in your goodness;
  in the greatness of your compassion wipe out my offense.
Thoroughly wash me from my guilt
  and of my sin cleanse me.
For I acknowledge my offense,
  and my sin is before me always:
"Against you only have I sinned,
  and done what is evil in your sight"—
That you may be justified in your sentence,
  vindicated when you condemn.
Indeed, in guilt was I born,
  and in sin my mother conceived me;
Behold, you are pleased with sincerity of heart,
  and in my inmost being you teach me wisdom.
Cleanse me of sin with hyssop, that I may be purified;
  wash me, and I shall be whiter than snow.
Let me hear the sounds of joy and gladness;
  the bones you have crushed shall rejoice.
Turn away your face from my sins,
  and blot out all my guilt.
A clean heart create for me, O God,
  and a steadfast spirit renew within me.
Cast me not out from your presence,
  and your holy spirit take not from me.
Give me back the joy of your salvation,
  and a willing spirit sustain in me.
I will teach transgressors your ways,
  and sinners will return to you.

Free me from blood guilt, O God, my saving God;
then my tongue shall revel in your justice.
O Lord, open my lips,
and my mouth shall proclaim your praise.
For you are not pleased with sacrifices;
should I offer a holocaust, you would not accept it.
My sacrifice, O God, is a contrite spirit;
a heart contrite and humbled, O God, you will not spurn.

(Psalm 50:1–19)

BRUCE VAWTER, C.M.

The Scriptural Meaning of Sin

The benevolent reader will find in this basic article a discussion of questions such as these: What is the most commonly used word for "sin" in the Old Testament and what does it mean? What is the meaning of sin in the Old Testament prophets? How did the notion of sin in the law relate to the covenant and to love? In what sense did the Old Testament think of sin as positive? What echo do we find in the Bible of the doctrine of temporal punishment due to sin? Why is sin an obstacle cutting man off from God? How do the Psalms speak of sin and justification? What is the difference between the New Testament and the Old Testament attitude toward sin? Why is sin an apostasy for the Christian?

Father Bruce Vawter is professor of Sacred Scripture at Kenrick Seminary in St. Louis, Missouri.

Etymologies are intriguing, though sometimes misleading, for it is use that really determines a word's meaning. But it is at least instructive to approach a term first through its etymology. When we do this with the words used in the Bible for sin, we find that none of

Reprinted with permission from *Theology Digest*, 10, 4 (Autumn 1962). The original article appeared as "Missing the Mark" in *The Way*, 2 (1962).

them has that exclusively moral association to which hundreds of years of Christianity have accustomed us.

In the Hebrew Old Testament the word most commonly used for sin is *ḥaṭṭah,* "to miss the mark," and the mark missed is not necessarily a moral one. Proverbs 19:2 uses this verb of the hasty traveler who loses his way through inadvertence to road signs. After *ḥaṭṭah,* the most commonly used Hebrew word for sin is *pesha,* "to overstep" or "to rebel." Here again we find no exclusively moral association; for instance, when 2 Kings 8:20 says Edom successfully "rebelled" against the rule of Juda, the author is passing no moral judgment on the revolt but simply recording a political fact. Nor do other Hebrew words that were used on occasion to signify a moral lapse have an exclusively moral application.

The Greek and Latin terms used to translate the Hebrew have much the same broad meaning. The Greek Old Testament renders *ḥaṭṭah* by *hamartano,* which also means "to miss the mark" and in profane Greek often refers to a man's losing his way on the road. In Latin, *peccare* has as its root meaning "to stumble" and did not originally connote anything moral. So etymology cannot tell us much about the biblical theology of sin.

We must, rather, see how the words are used, as we said at the beginning. A legalistic interpretation of biblical religion could make the notion of sin something purely formal: not a matter of rightdoing but rather of the avoidance of wrongdoing. But Wellhausen was certainly wrong in extending such a conception to the law itself and to the way it was understood in the biblical period. This can be clarified by examining a few passages.

Usage in the Prophets

See, for example, the prophet Amos's use of *pesha.* The "transgressions" of which he speaks include inhumanity, cruelty, social injustice, violation of contract, acceptance of bribes, violation of public trust, greed, lust, and hypocrisy, on the part of the Gentiles as well as of the Israelites (Am 1:3; 2:8). There is obviously no question here of sin as the merely formal, mechanically computed violation of law. For Amos *pesha* is a rebellion against God's moral will, which is known to Jew and Gentile alike as the norm of rightdoing. It is true that Amos does not elaborate a doctrine of natural law, but he does say (6:12) that the rejection of the justice and the rightdoing that God required of Israel was as absurd and unnatural as tracking horses over rocks and ploughing the sea with oxen. Sin for the Israelite was the violated will and law of the Lord, but it was a will and law that found a response in man's mind and heart; it was never arbitrary whim or caprice.

This meaning of *pesha* that we first find in Amos is also common to the rest of the prophets. And it is proper to look in the prophets for an expression of the spirit of the law. The criticism of the past century tried to oppose the two, as though the spiritual, prophetic religion and the priestly religion of the law had been separate, antagonistic developments in Israelite history. We now recognize that in this attempt the critics had also taken the wrong track and missed the mark. Prophecy and law are, of course, two different emphases of Israelite religion, which spoke two different languages. But they were emphases of the same religion and were directed toward more or less the same ends. We do not expect to find the moral and devotional teaching of Catholicism in the Code of Canon Law or the Roman Ritual. Similarly, it is now agreed that we rightly interpret prophetic teaching in the Old Testament as supporting in its way a doctrine that the law upheld in its way.

Meaning in the Law

In the law the favored word for sin was *hattah,* and the "mark" that was missed was that of the Covenant of Sinai. Israel's law was the spelling out of the people's obligations with respect to this covenant, so we must have a clear idea of what covenant meant in the ancient Near East. Whereas the binding force of an ordinary contract is based on legal justice, a covenant obligation was not thought of primarily as one of justice but as one of love. The word customarily used in the Old Testament for the notion of the covenant bond is *hesed,* which may mean mercy, loyalty, devotion, loving kindness, or simply love. The covenant idea was modeled after a familial rather than a legal relationship. When an Israelite committed *hattah* (sinned), his offense was not determined by the letter of the law he had violated but by the familial piety he had ruptured.

Sin Is Positive

To the Semite, sin and evil were not negative (the deprivation of good) but something positive that had been done and that continued to exist until done away with. What we consider "guilt" and "punishment" were to the biblical authors hardly distinguishable from the sin itself. In Numbers 32:23, for instance, we translate the same Hebrew word as both "sin" and "consequences of sin." Because sin was seen as something positive, even those sins committed in ignorance demanded expiatory rites and sacrifices, and whole communities, yet unborn, could share in the guilt of the progenitor or of a fellow member. It was not that they were held "guilty" of another's wrongdoing; they were simply caught up in the consequences of an act in a situation where the consequences were the continued existence of the act itself.

Similarly, punishment was not so much a retribution visited upon the sin as it was the inexorable running of sin's course. God could forestall this consequence—by accepting sacrifices for sins of ignorance and responding to prayer, sorrow, and confession for other sins. But God's forgiveness of sin did not automatically entail his remission of punishment, as can be seen from the famous judgment passed on David's sin with Bathsheba. Catholic teaching on the temporal punishment of sin is a true echo of this biblical doctrine.

We can see from this "objective" view of sin in the Old Testament why what was sinful was broader in extent than what was immoral. Legal purity, which was the external holiness of a people consecrated to God and a reminder of their need for interior holiness, could be violated without any immoral act. A woman had to make a "guilt offering" after childbirth, for instance, even though no question of morality was involved. In this there is a major difference between the Old and New Testaments, for we find in the New Testament no trace of the idea of purely legal holiness. The old formulas are used, but within the new dimension of a salvation and regeneration of which the former figures were but a foreshadowing. The "holy ones" to whom St. Paul writes are those of whom personal holiness is expected as a consequence of the indwelling Spirit. With the entire apparatus of formal sanctity superseded in a new and spiritual covenant, sin and immorality are fully identified. The law of Christians is the code of conduct of a people which has charity as the *hesed* of their covenant with God.

Another consequence of the objective view of sin in the Old Testament is that it is represented as an obstacle that stands between God and his people. Expiation is the removal of this obstacle; it is not a matter of "appeasing" God or changing him in any way but of removing the sin from man. If a sin has been willful, the mind and heart must be changed by repentance. In Isaia 6 we see how clearly the prophet sees sin as such a cutting off of man from God; man is "lost" in the presence of the Holy. Perhaps the same idea is present in the English word "sin," namely that it "sunders" one from the other (as in the German *Sünde*).

Psalmist's Notions

From the penitential psalms, and notably from Psalm 50, the *Miserere*, we gain an even clearer idea of the biblical theology of sin. Three different words are used to express what the sinner begs God to do for him in his sinful state: "blot out," "wash," and "cleanse." All three verbs denote a ritual or declaratory obliteration of sin, but we must recall that the "washing" the second verb alludes to is the washing of clothes—and the oriental flung his soiled clothing in a stream and stomped on it enthusiastically. So the psalmist is asking God for two kinds of cleaning—what a later theology will distinguish into a forensic and a real justification.

In the *forensic* justification, God simply declares the sinner to be a sinner no more. But since it is obvious that no human act can be done away with as though it had never occurred, there must also be a *real* justification. The guilt that has remained in the sinner and prevents his access to the God of holiness must be stamped out and obliterated, like the dirt in a soiled robe. The psalmist calls on the Lord to "create a clean heart" and to "renew an upright spirit" within him. For the Israelite, the "heart" was the seat of all emotion, will, and thought; he thought or "said" things in his heart, not in his mind. And the "spirit" was the power that God put in man to enable him to think and will in his heart. So we see that for the psalmist the justification of the sinner entailed a divine work of recreation, a renewal of a personality that had been distorted and turned aside from its true purposes by the act of sin. Create, he says, a new *me*. Sin was, in his eyes, an involvement from which man could not emerge without an alteration in his inmost being.

The Old Testament background of St. Paul's doctrine of original sin can be seen in Psalm 50:7, "Behold, I was brought forth in guilt, and in sin my mother conceived me." The psalmist says this as a motivation to God to be merciful, as a reminder that man's proclivities are sinful. Biblical authors knew well that the introduction of sin into the world and its continuation were the achievement of human malice against the will of God. Man's disposition to sin was part of a consistent history in which the will of a saving God had been resisted and thwarted from the first.

New Testament Emphasis

Most of the Old Testament theology of sin can be found in the thinking of the New Testament authors, but there is also a decisive difference that results from the new and definitive revelation of Christianity. For while sin was taken for granted and elaborately provided for in the life of the Old Covenant, the New Testament Church saw in itself the fulfillment of the prophets' prediction of a new and everlasting covenant in which sin would have no part. Sin was, therefore, always a kind of apostasy for the Christian. Because the Christian could always relapse into his old ways, sin was an ever present possibility. Yet he could sin only by abandoning the total commitment involved in Christian faith, which he could regain only through the new heart and spirit that must once more be bestowed on him by divine grace.

The sense of horror and of enormity in the presence of sin never deserts the New Testament. If we today can summon a somewhat casual attitude to the function of the confessional in the sacramental life of the Church, undoubtedly this is partly due to the fact that modern man, even Christian man, has to a greater or less extent forgotten what sin really is. Probably man can never really lose his sense of sin, though today he seems to have great difficulty in defining for himself what he means by it. When we look about us at a world in which men give witness to a feeling of rootless and purposeless existence, to a life bereft of meaningful experience in which event follows event in witless sequence and where men can achieve no community together, we perceive in a groping sort of way what biblical man understood by sin.

III. FAITH

The Word of God

Brethren, my heart's desire and my prayer to God is in their behalf unto their salvation. For I bear them witness that they have zeal for God, but not according to knowledge; for, ignorant of the justice of God, and seeking to establish their own, they have not submitted to the justice of God. For Christ is the consummation of the Law unto justice for everyone who believes.

For Moses wrote that the man who does that justice which is of the Law shall live by it. But the justice that is of faith says, "Do not say in thy heart: Who shall ascend into heaven?" (that is, to bring down Christ); or, "Who shall descend into the abyss?" (that is, to bring up Christ from the dead). But what does it say? "The word is near thee, in thy mouth and in thy heart" (that is, the word of faith, which we preach). For if thou confess with thy mouth that Jesus is the Lord, and believe in thy heart that God has raised him from the dead, thou shalt be saved. For with the heart a man believes unto justice, and with the mouth profession of faith is made unto salvation. For the Scripture says, "Whoever believes in him shall not be disappointed." For there is no distinction between Jew and Greek, for there is the same Lord of all, rich towards all who call upon him. "For whoever calls upon the name of the Lord shall be saved."

How then are they to call upon him in whom they have not believed? But how are they to believe him whom they have not heard? And how are they to hear, if no one preaches? And how are men to preach unless they be sent? As it is written,

*"How beautiful are the feet of those who preach the gospel of peace;
Of those who bring glad tidings of good things!"*

But all did not obey the gospel. For Isaia says,
"Lord, who has believed our report?"
Faith then depends on hearing, and hearing on the word of Christ.
But I say: Have they not heard? Yes, indeed,
"Their voice has gone forth into all the earth,
And their words unto the ends of the world."

(Romans 10:1–18)

BRUCE VAWTER, C.M.

The Biblical Idea of Faith

The conscientious reader will find in this short essay a discussion of questions such as these: What are the varied notions that the words faith and belief convey to the Semitic mind? How are these notions transferred to the New Testament? Does the biblical idea of faith exclude an intellectual element? How does faith involve the will? The whole man? How does the New Testament describe various degrees of faith? What is unique about Christian revelation that gives a special dimension to faith? Why was Paul correct in affirming that faith justifies? What did he mean by faith in this connection? Does the faith that justifies refer more to the future or to what is actual and real? Why was the question of "faith versus works" in the sixteenth century a false issue? What is the difference between fideism and faith?

Father Bruce Vawter, author of a previous article, is the author of A Path Through Genesis and The Conscience of Israel.

In the course of his Bamptom Lectures of 1938, Professor Alfred Guillaume has included the eyewitness account of a vindication by ordeal as still practiced, as a last resort, among certain Bedouin

This article appeared in *Worship*, Collegeville, Minn. (August–September 1960). It was reprinted in *Guide* (May 1961) and is reproduced here with permission.

tribes of Arabia. In this particular ordeal, a white-hot spoon was licked three times by the accused, with the result that nothing more than a touch of dry ash was found on his tongue, though it has been known for men to lose the whole or a part of their tongues in such experiments. As Guillaume concludes:

This ordeal, from its beginning to its end, is based on the belief that God will vindicate the innocent and punish the guilty, and though it is so ancient that it cannot be used as an argument for the truth of the central dogma of religion which Jews, Christians, and Muhammadans hold in common, it has real value as a demonstration of what a Semitic people understand by faith.

What a Semitic people understand by faith is, of course, also what the Bible understands by faith.

Things are usually what they are said to be: *nomen est omen,* said the ancients. It is doubtless due in part to our deriving our word "faith" from *fidere,* "confide in," "credit," that we tend to think of it as pretty much exclusively concerned with the mind. It is not quite the same, I think, with our verb "believe," which we use to indicate the exercise of faith.

"Believe," which is cognate with words used in other Germanic languages for "faith" (*Glaube, geloof*), is related to the obsolete verb "belove," found now only in the passive. When we say, therefore, that we believe—or, to be sure, when our ancestors said it—we express much more than a mere intellectual assent. We express commitment, engagement, that giving over of the whole self that is entailed in what we call "love."

By a kindred association of ideas, the biblical authors indicated much the same thing as their understanding of faith. The Hebrew words which we translate "fidelity," "faith," and also "truth," are all derived from the verb *aman,* which has the meaning "be firm, sure." We are all quite familiar with one form of this word, the liturgical affirmation "amen," which is to say "this is most certain." To signify belief in someone or something, Hebrew uses a causal form of this verb ("make firm") together with the preposition "in" or "to."

Scholars are not fully agreed what was the underlying thought-pattern, whether the person conceived himself as being made strong in relation to the object of his faith, or whether he declared this object of faith a firm foundation. In either case, it is plain that in this Semitic acceptance there is a more personal involvement than is really adequately described in terms of "subject" and "object." In faith, one does not merely accept a proposition, he sets his whole being in relation to another.

This Semitic idea of faith is also that of the New Testament. The writers of the New Testament preached a faith which had a new content and new direction, but which was in nature the same. What the Old Testament Israelite had professed with regard to Yahweh, in the New Testament was a profession of the Holy Trinity and of the Lord Jesus.

An engagement of the entire person involves, naturally, intellectual assent. As has just been noted, there has been a Western tendency to emphasize the intellectual side of faith. Apart from the reason I suggested, there have been good historical causes for this emphasis: the anti-intellectualism of the Reformation was one, and in more recent times Modernism's subjectivism has been another, both of which encouraged us to insist on the objective reasonableness of the act of faith.

Such an emphasis also has authentic biblical roots. The Jews at various times, particularly in their contacts with the intellectual ferment of Hellenism, were impelled to the same emphasis, as were the writers of the New Testament. No one who reads the biblical authors without prejudice could ever think that for them faith is anything short of an act in which the human mind, far from abdicating its office, is performing what is most worthy of it, wholly in keeping with its nature and dignity.

But the isolation of man's mind, after all, however useful to the philosopher in the analysis of a human act, is not a reality in everyday doings. "After all," as Newman rightly said, "man is *not* a reasoning animal; he is a seeing, feeling, contemplating, acting animal." What engages his faith is not what engages his mind only, or what he may apprehend primarily in intellectual terms.

He is more apt to believe "in his bones," as we say, or "in his heart of hearts." The absolute and irrevocable commitment that is expressed in martyrdom we do not think of primarily as an intellectual act, though of course it is that ultimately. We think of it, and the martyr thinks of it, as an act of faith performed by his whole being.

Catholic theology has always avoided what is sometimes implied, unfortunately, in some of our popular treatments of faith, which might give the impression that it is (as the Book of Common Prayer called it) a "persuasion," merely the inheritance of a traditional body of doctrine.

A Personal Encounter

Theology has always insisted that faith is a personal encounter of the believer with the first, the divine truth. It has always stressed the intervention of the human will in the act of faith: precisely because faith is faith, and not knowledge, the will must command the assent of the mind. *Credo quia impossibile*—"I believe because it is impossible," may or may not have been said by the Church Fathers, but whether said or not, it expresses—taken rightly, of course—a truth proper to faith, which is not anti-intellectual but super-intellectual.

That faith is the act of the whole man, not only of his mind, explains the Church's traditional horror of the heretic, a horror so difficult to explain nowadays to those for whom faith is the equivalent of opinion. Goodness and malice reside in the will, not the intellect. A heretic, in the true sense of the word, is not one who merely shares an erroneous conclusion about what is revealed truth, as saints and even Doctors of the Church have done. He is, rather, one who has willfully cut himself loose from the Author of his supernatural existence.

When the writer of Hebrews says that "it is impossible to bring back to repentance those who were once enlightened, who have tasted the heavenly gift, who have been made partakers of the Holy Spirit, who have tasted the good word of God and the power of the world to come, and then have fallen away," he says what every pastor of souls knows by daily experience. And he knows equally well the reason: "For they have again crucified for themselves the Son of God and held him up to mockery" (Heb 6:4–6). How often—and how often vainly—have we reasoned with the "fallen away" about his abandonment of the faith! And how often is anything intellectual really involved? An apostate has not changed his mind only, he has wrenched his entire person into a new, and wrong, direction.

"Of Small Faith"

Our Lord's frequent rebuke of his disciples as *oligopistoi*, "of small faith" (Mt 6:30; 8:26, etc.), evidently was not to question how much they believed statistically, but how deeply. They believed, but not consistently, not wholeheartedly, not with complete commitment.

They were what the father of the boy whose cure is described in Mark 9:13–28 humbly confessed to be: "I believe; come to the aid of my unbelief"—meaning, as Father Lagrange has pointed out: "come to my aid, even though I do not believe strongly enough." Similarly, when our Lord said of the centurion, "such faith I have found with no one in Israel" (Mt 8:10), the sting of the comparison derives from the fact that the uncircumcised centurion, greatly at a disadvantage in respect to his acceptance of formal revelation, nevertheless displayed better than the recipients of that revelation the attitude of soul which in the Bible means faith.

Anyone who has read the New Testament knows how much broader is the scope of "faith" than that which we are apt to give it. Often the New Testament word will have to be translated, or at least understood by us, now as "confidence," now "trust," now "hope," now "conviction," now "assent," and even, as St. Paul uses it in Romans 14:22, something like "informed conscience."

It is well to remember, however, that these distinctions are ours, in accordance with a psychological view of man that is not found in the New Testament. The distinctions may be very useful, even necessary to our thinking, but neither should we permit ourselves to become the victims of our own method. We should not lose sight of the fact that to the authors of the New Testament revelation, who had one word for all these things, faith was such an all-embracing idea.

Though the New Testament authors inherited their idea of faith from the Old Testament, faith itself has a far greater significance in the New Testament than it ever did in the Old. This is the result not only of the new revelation which had made better known than ever before the extent of the tremendous mysteries of God. Even more importantly, it is the result of an entirely new dimension given to faith in God's ultimate revelation of himself in his only Son.

The newness of this dimension is strikingly reflected in the expression, common in John's Gospel, but likewise found throughout the New Testament, "believe *into* Christ (or God)." This formula, impossible to reproduce in good English, has been preserved in our creeds, where *Credo in Deum* is a strictly Christian form, replacing the *Credo Deum* or *Deo* of classical Latin. Scholars are agreed that this unusual terminology reflects the new theological thinking of the primitive Christian Church.

Christian Revelation Unique

It is not simply an imitation of the Old Testament formula mentioned above (the preposition "in" with the verb *aman*), for the Greek Old Testament on which the New Testament writers largely depend for their theological language had never tried to reproduce this Semitic idiom in Greek. It is, rather, an attempt to express the unique character of the Christian revelation, which is essentially of a Person. St. Thomas caught the drift of this formula in Scholastic terms when he wrote that *credere in Deum* properly expresses the act of faith as commanded by the will, since the will inclines to the divine truth as to its end (*Summa*, II–II, 2, 2).

In the New Testament God, or Christ, is much more personally the object of faith than in the Old Testament. There is, in a sense, less to believe "about" him, since he is now apprehended personally, who is the end of our natural and supernatural being. The word of God made known in the fragmentary utterances of the Old Testament is in the New Testament possessed incarnate.

Christian faith is not just a means to God, "a shadow of the good things to come," but the possession of God and his divine Son.

It is this personal direction of Christian faith which explains the Pauline formula "faith of Jesus," that is, "faith which is (of) Jesus," the equivalent of "faith in Jesus." John contrasts the mediacy of Old Testament religion with the immediate possession of divine life shared by those who have faith in Christ: "The Law was given through Moses, while grace and truth have come through Jesus Christ" (1:18). "He has given them the power to become sons of God, those who believe *into* his name" (1:12). This is real, not merely imputed sonship (cf. 1 Jn 3:1), as real as the Christ to whom we are joined by faith.

Because of the object of Christian faith, it becomes clear how Paul can regard it as justifying. In his famous teaching on justification by faith the Apostle builds on Genesis 15:6, where it is said that Abraham "believed (in) God, who accounted it in him as righteousness."

Under the influence of a growing legalism, the rabbis in their exegesis of this text completely turned it against its evident meaning, taking Abraham's faith as a prescribed work for which he had been rewarded. To support this construction, they evolved the fantastic legend that the whole of the Mosaic Law had been revealed to

Abraham. His act of faith was a fulfillment of the Law. "The merit of Abraham" was a rabbinical description of the episode of Genesis 15. Paul's teaching obviously polemizes against this idea, to the glorification of Christian faith.

Justification, says Paul, is God's free gift, "according to grace." In this Abraham became the father of all who believe, that his faith was accounted justice in him, just as our faith is accounted justice in us, coming from the gratuitous act of God's mercy in saving us from sin through Jesus Christ. The text of Genesis—in its real meaning, not in the interpretation of the rabbis—signified that Abraham's faith was accepted by God as possessing a value it did not have of itself: such is the sense of the Hebrew word used for "account."

In virtue of Abraham's faith, God justified him, accounted him righteous, bestowed on him His friendship and thus endowed him with a righteousness he could not have had of himself. Such was the value of Old Testament faith, and such is the effect of Christian faith, but to the latter Paul ascribes even more, in keeping with the new dimension of faith.

For Christian faith is directed not to a promise, but to a fulfilled reality. By Christian faith we are not only united to a God who promises, as he did to Abraham, but to him "who has raised Jesus our Lord from the dead, who was delivered up for our sins and rose again for our justification" (Rom 4:25). Our justification from faith (5:1) results in our now having reconciliation (5:11). Faith in him who raised Jesus is also faith in Jesus himself: "We have also believed in Christ Jesus, that we may be justified by the faith of Christ" (Gal 2:16).

Christian faith, in other words, actually is righteousness, since it connects the believer with the source of his salvation. Hence St. Thomas in his commentary on Romans 4:5 observes that the justice accounted to the believer is "not indeed that by faith he merits justice, but belief itself is the first act of justice which God works in him. For inasmuch as he believes in God who justifies, he submits himself to His justification, and thus receives its effect."

Total Commitment

This justifying faith, in Genesis and in St. Paul and in St. Thomas, is more than an assent to a truth. It is a total acceptance of *the* truth, who is God, even against every human consideration, a wholehearted commitment which is the beginning of a new way of life. "He did not waver through lack of faith concerning the promise of God, but he grew strong in faith giving glory to God, fully convinced that he was able to do what he had promised. Therefore it was accounted to him as righteousness" (Rom 4:20–22).

It is equally plain from the teaching of the New Testament that the faith *versus* works controversy posed by the Reformation was a false issue. Faith is both something less and something more than the early Reformers taught, in proportion as the righteousness achieved through faith is a reality and not the imputation that they believed. What God declares, is. "God gives life to the dead and calls into being things that were not" (Rom 4:17). Because faith is a commitment of life, not just a frame of mind, it necessarily entails good works. Because the justification of faith is real, the works of faith also God accounts as righteousness.

Admittedly the epistle of James begins from a different standpoint than Paul's, but there is no conflict in its complement of the Pauline doctrine of justification: "Was not Abraham our father justified by works, when he offered Isaac his son on the altar? You see that faith worked together with his works, and by works faith was made complete. Thus the Scripture was fulfilled: 'Abraham believed God, and it was accounted to him as righteousness,' and he was called the friend of God. You see that a man is justified by works, and not from faith only" (Jas 2:21–24).

It is just as important today as it has been in the past for us to lay stress on the objectivity and the reasonableness of faith, to lay stress, therefore, on its intellectual aspect. The concept of faith professed by existentialist theologians like Rudolf Bultmann, rejecting as it does all objectivity, all motives of credibility, all verification of historical revelation, is less acceptable to Catholics than the original ideas of primitive Protestantism. This is fideism rather than faith, a concept hardly to be ascribed to the New Testament whose authors were the heirs and witnesses of a continuity of divine revelation within history.

At the same time, however, when Bultmann and others speak of the here-and-nowness of faith, they are on firm biblical ground. If our faith is not our way of life, the principle of our every action, our very life with God, then we do not understand faith as the Bible understands it.

It is not enough that we "make an act of faith" in the divine mysteries, we must *believe* them. It is not enough that we believe that Jesus Christ was raised from the dead, we must believe *in* the resurrected Christ. It is by such faith that the New Testament teaches Christians to live in this life, till faith yields to vision.

IV. JUSTICE

The Word of God

On that day they will sing this song in the land of Juda: "A strong city have we; he sets up walls and ramparts to protect us. Open up the gates to let in a nation that is just, one that keeps faith. A nation of firm purpose you keep in peace; in peace, for its trust in you."

Trust in the Lord forever! For the Lord is an eternal Rock. He humbles those in high places, and the lofty city he brings down; he tumbles it to the ground, levels it with the dust. It is trampled underfoot by the needy, by the footsteps of the poor.

The way of the just is smooth; the path of the just you make level. Yes, for your way and your judgments, O Lord, we look to you; your name and your title are the desire of our souls. My soul yearns for you in the night, yes, my spirit within me keeps vigil for you; when your judgment dawns upon the earth, the world's inhabitants learn justice. The wicked man, spared, does not learn justice; in an upright land he acts perversely, and sees not the majesty of the Lord. O Lord, your hand is uplifted, but they behold it not; let them be shamed when they see your zeal for your people: let the fire prepared for your enemies consume them. O Lord, you mete out peace to us, for it is you who have accomplished all we have done. O Lord, our God, other lords than you have ruled us; it is from you only that we can call upon your name.

Dead they are, they have no life, shades that cannot rise; for you have punished and destroyed them, and wiped out all memory of them. You have increased the nation, O Lord, increased the nation to your own glory, and extended far all the borders of the land. O Lord, oppressed by your punishment, we cried out in *anguish under your chastising. As a woman about to give birth writhes and cries out in her pains, so were we in your presence, O Lord.*

We conceived and writhed in pain, giving birth to wind; salvation we have not achieved for the earth, the inhabitants of the world cannot bring it forth. But your dead shall live, their corpses shall rise; awake and sing, you who lie in the dust. For your dew is a dew of light, and the land of shades gives birth.

(Isaia 26:1–19)

JEAN DANIÉLOU

The Justice of God

The dutiful reader will find in this significant excerpt from a chapter called "The God of the Faith" a discussion of questions such as these: Why is it important to understand a biblical category such as *tsedeq?* How did the ancient Greeks and Romans think of justice? Could God be condemned before a tribunal of justice so conceived? How would the "justification" of God in these terms lead to dangerous consequences in theory and practice? How does God's justice differ radically from commutative justice? Why were the Pharisees wrong in demanding their rights before God? In what sense is God just? What is the "justice" that Christ came to establish on earth? How is justice eschatological? How is God's justice complete in Christ? How is God's justice the measure of man's? How can the biblical notion of God's justice serve as the basis for human justice and respect for the rights of individuals?

Father Jean Daniélou is a professor of the Faculty of Theology of Paris. He is also the author of *Christ and Us, Origen,* and many other works.

From *God and the Ways of Knowing* by Jean Daniélou. Copyright © 1957 by Meridian Books, Inc. Reprinted by arrangement with The World Publishing Company, Cleveland and New York. A Meridian Book.

The problem of God's justice raises similar questions to that of his truth. Here again we are in the presence of an idea borrowed from current language, which in this case served to translate a biblical category, the *tsedeq*. For lack of a precise study of this word, and therefore of the word "justice" in biblical usage, we see what confusion we are in danger of incurring. Moreover, the existence of these confusions is not a myth. How many social theories have claimed the authority of that saying of Christ: "Blessed are they which do hunger and thirst after justice"! What confused ideas are suggested to the majority of minds by a sentence like: "Seek ye first the kingdom of heaven and its justice"! Lack of precision in elucidating these basic categories of biblical theology may have the gravest consequences. This is why we think it worthwhile to emphasize such points.

Among the ancients we find a current conception of justice. The Greeks call it *dikè*, the Latins *iustitia*. Its essential purpose is to insure that the right, *ius*, of everyone should be respected, that everyone should have rendered to him what is his due. This justice is the foundation of human societies. It is also the imperious demand of the human soul. (Nothing shocks a child more than injustice.) It easily takes the form of an equalitarian claim, in protest against the inequality of conditions and as a demand that all should be treated equally. In every way, it seems to require that there should be a due proportion between merit and retribution.

But if we confront the reality of the world with this conception of justice, we are compelled to state that it implies a complete contradiction. I am not thinking here of social injustices, for which the responsibility can be allotted to man, but of what one may call natural injustices. How can we speak of justice in a world where some children are born weak and others with every advantage, where there are innocent people overwhelmed with misfortune and criminals flourishing with impunity? If we apply to such a world the criteria of human justice, and if we summon God before the tribunal of that justice, he could not but be condemned. This is what rightly makes an author like Camus refuse to accept a world constructed in such a way, for he can see no other answer to it than revolt.

Attempts to justify God seem still more perilous, for they end inevitably in a checkmate. How can we dare to claim that there is a relationship between virtue and goodness, between vice and misfortune, when the contradictions are so glaring? Moreover, the Bible itself has refused in advance, through the mouth of Job, all attempts of this kind. They end, besides, in the worst Pharisaism. For if prosperity necessarily accompanies virtue, it is also its criterion, and the fortunate of this world could then settle down with a good conscience and calmly despise the unfortunate, regarding their misery as a just punishment. In the practical sphere, the triumph of force would be identified with the triumph of right, and the conquered people would necessarily be the guilty people. We see the dangerous providentialism to which all this would lead.

But at the bottom of this there is a fundamental ambiguity. For God's justice, according to the Bible, has nothing in common with the commutative justice that governs relationships between men, and the mistake lies precisely in wishing to apply such a criterion to the relationship between God and men. If the facts themselves were not already startling enough to arouse our suspicions and put us on our guard against an immediate scandal, the teachings of the Gospel would be sufficient to enlighten us in this matter. A parable like that of the workmen in the last hour is indeed a flat contradiction of the human conception of justice, and constitutes in man's eyes a complete outrage. It puts forward in principle the right of God to treat men with the most perfect inequality, and without taking any account of the difference between their respective rights.

But what Christ meant to show us here is precisely that the fundamental error in our idea of the relationship between man and God was to imagine that man had any rights before God whatever. This was the mistake of the Pharisees, who claimed to be treated according to their merits and brought their demands before God. But it is this claim on the part of man that must be entirely overruled. Man has nothing except what he receives as a completely free gift, and he therefore has nothing at all on which he could base a claim. Accordingly he cannot complain if he is treated differently from others. God demands sovereign freedom in the designations of his gifts. Perhaps in the end we shall be "up on the deal," and it would be better for us in the last resort to put our trust in merciful love, rather than to make a stand on our supposed merits.

But shall we not fall into the opposite idea of an arbitrary God? The Bible teaches us just the reverse. What it denounces is man's claim to judge according to the standards of his own justice. We come back to what we said above on the subject of reason. A God who was just, after the style of man, would not be the transcendent, hidden God. But there *is* justice in God. That justice, if it is at first disconcerting for man, if it seems strange to him and stupefies him, is in reality wholly excellent. The God of the Bible thus forces man to leave his own ways, which are short and narrow, and enter the ways of God, which are infinitely wiser and more merciful. This requires of him that conversion, that decentralization from himself, which is—as we have already stated several times—the very sign of an encounter with the living God.

It is this justice of God which is the *tsedeq* of the Bible. It does not consist of the fact that God owes something to man, but in what he owes to himself. Justice is thus a continuation of truth. It consists for God of keeping his commitments and thus showing his faithfulness. It is the fulfillment of his promises that attests God's justice. This is how we should interpret certain otherwise obscure passages in the New Testament. When Christ says that he came to fulfill all justice, this does not mean that he came to establish a just wage or a just peace, but to keep the promises made to Abraham by saving captive humanity. When Christ tells us that the Comforter "will convince the world of sin, and of justice, and of judgment . . . because I go to my Father" (Jn 16:8–10), he means that by his glorious exaltation he reveals the success of the divine plan and denounces the error of those who have not believed in him.

Justice often presents in this way an eschatological character. If truth accompanies the promise, justice appears in its fulfillment. It provides a verification. It is in this sense that justice draws near to the kingdom as an object of expectation, and it is in this sense that we should understand texts like: "Blessed are they which do hunger and thirst after justice." This means that those who have believed in the divine promises are finally right and will see them fulfilled. So also when Christ tells his followers to "seek the kingdom of heaven and its justice." Justice and the kingdom are one and the same thing. They are the order of things in which God's plan triumphs. So again when it is a question of those who "are persecuted for justice's sake." God's justice is not defined with reference to man. It is the faithfulness of love to itself. We see from this why the order that it establishes is better. To believe that God is just, is to believe that it is he who will finally be right, despite all appearances, that he will make his cause prevail, that "He will be the strongest," as Claudel's Joan of Arc says—and that he will thus insure the well-being of those who have believed in him.

God's justice is completed in Jesus Christ, for it is in him that God fulfills his promise. This dominates the whole Christian outlook, which is faith in a salvation freely given to sinners and not legally merited by the just: "But now the justice of God without the law is made manifest . . . upon all them that believe in him: for there is no distinction: for all have sinned, and do need the glory of God; being justified freely by his grace, through the redemption, that is in Christ Jesus" (Rom 3:21-24). God's justice, far from being proportioned to human merits, is shown on the contrary, as St. Paul says, by the fact that God has declared his justice "for the remissions of former sins" (Rom 3:25), that the success of his plan is not at the mercy of man—and that the condition on which we may benefit from it is faith.

Thus man's righteousness is not the condition, but the consequence of God's action. It is this alone that justifies. The righteous man is he whom God declares and renders such. It is God's justice that thus provides the measure of man's, and not the other way about. The only thing that is required of man is faith. But the faith of which St. Paul speaks is not what Luther wished it to mean. It is not only confidence in the justice of God, in his ultimate victory, but the conforming of one's life to the will of God. It is not enough to be baptized in order to be saved, any more than it was enough to belong to the people of Israel in order to enter into their inheritance. But the righteous man is he in whom is found justification by the fruits of life and by holiness, and who thus bears witness to a justice that does not derive from himself, but comes from God. He is not only one who believes in the fulfillment of promises, but is one in whom they are fulfilled.

Thus we are brought back to the popular idea of justice, insofar as it expresses in human relationships a respect for the rights of the individual. We have said that biblical justice had in substance nothing in common with human justice, and this is quite true. But biblical justice implies, nevertheless, the duty of man to respect and promote the person of his fellow-man. Only this obligation does not proceed ultimately from the rights of persons as such, but from the fact that this respect for persons is the expression of the will of God. It is, then, obedience to God, the acknowledgment of the charter of the covenant, that implies a certain order of human society. Here again, justice will be defined, not by reference to the claims of man, but to the will of God. This is why Christian justice must surpass that of the scribes and Pharisees, in that it is identified with charity.

V. WISDOM

The Word of God

My son, if you receive my words
   and treasure my commands,
Turning your ear to wisdom,
   inclining your heart to understanding;
Yes, if you call to intelligence,
   and to understanding raise your voice;
If you seek her like silver,
   and like hidden treasures search her out:
Then will you understand the fear of the Lord:
   the knowledge of God you will find;
For the Lord gives wisdom,
   from his mouth comes knowledge and understanding;
He has counsel in store for the upright,
   he is the shield of those who walk honestly,
Guarding the paths of justice,
   protecting the way of his pious ones.
Then you will understand rectitude and justice,
   honesty, every good path;
For wisdom will enter your heart,
   knowledge will please your soul,
Discretion will watch over you,
   understanding will guard you;
Saving you from the way of evil men,
   from men of perverse speech,
Who leave the straight paths
   to walk in ways of darkness,
Who delight in doing evil,
   rejoice in perversity;

Whose ways are crooked,
  and devious their paths;
Saving you from the wife of another,
  from the adulteress with her smooth words,
Who forsakes the companion of her youth
  and forgets the pact with her God;
For her path sinks down to death,
  and her footsteps lead to the shades;
None who enter thereon come back again,
  or gain the paths of life.
Thus you may walk in the way of good men,
  and keep to the paths of the just.
For the upright will dwell in the land,
  the honest will remain in it;
But the wicked will be cut off from the land,
  the faithless will be rooted out of it.

(Proverbs 2:1–22)

BERNHARD ANDERSON

Human and Divine Wisdom
in Proverbs

The eager reader will find in this concise analysis a discussion of questions such as these: How diversified are the collections represented in the book of Proverbs? How are the proverbs constructed? Are they concerned with purely religious matters? How do they relate to religious faith? What is the meaning and importance of the saying that "the fear of the Lord is the beginning of wisdom"?

Reprinted with permission from Chapter 15, "The Beginning of Wisdom," in Bernhard W. Anderson, *Understanding the Old Testament* (Englewood Cliffs, N.J.: Prentice-Hall, Inc., 1957).

How is the wisdom tradition related to the prophets? How does the Book of Proverbs relate human wisdom to divine wisdom? How are the wise contrasted with the foolish?

Dr. Bernhard Anderson is Dean of the Theological School of Drew University and the author of Understanding the Old Testament, from which this excerpt was taken.

An Anthology of Proverbs

The history of Israel's wisdom movement is condensed in the pages of the book of Proverbs. It is generally agreed that this book, in its final form, comes from the period of Judaism, probably after the time of Ezra, when the wisdom schools were flourishing. But like the Pentateuch, the book of Proverbs represents the final stage of a tradition that goes back at least to the time of Solomon, who may have composed or collected the original nucleus. As the following headings indicate, several wisdom collections are contained in this one book:

1. Chs. 1–9: "The proverbs of Solomon"
2. 10:1–22:16: "The proverbs of Solomon"
3. 22:17–24:22: "The words of the Wise"
   24:23–34: "These also are sayings of the Wise"
4. Chs. 25–29: "The proverbs of Solomon collected by the men of king Hezekiah"
5. Ch. 30: "The words of Agur the son of Jakeh"
6. 31:1–9: "The words of Lemuel king of Massa"
7. 31:10–31: An alphabetic poem on the good housewife

A glance at this material is enough to show the diversity of the book. Notice that, in general, numbers 1–4 belong to the tradition of Solomon, while the remainder of the book is of foreign origin. And within these four, most scholars regard the second collection as the oldest portion of the book of Proverbs. The first collection is often regarded as the latest, but in view of the Canaanite elements in this section some scholars regard at least part of it as belonging to the pre-exilic tradition. All we can say for sure is that the book of Proverbs represents a complex tradition, extending throughout almost the whole of the Old Testament period.

Common-Sense Proverbs

The wisdom sayings of this anthology are usually short, crisp, two-line sentences dealing with some aspect of experience. In some instances, the second line of the proverb runs parallel to the thought of the first. An example of this "synonymous parallelism" is found in Proverbs 22:1:

> A good name is to be chosen rather than great riches,
> and favor is better than silver and gold.

Often the lines are a balanced pair of opposites. This type of "antithetic parallelism" is illustrated by 10:1:

> A wise son makes a glad father,
> but a foolish son is a sorrow to his mother.

And sometimes the second line of the pair completes the thought of the first, in a kind of "ascending parallelism," as in 11:22:

> Like a gold ring in a swine's snout
> is a beautiful woman without discretion.

Many of the proverbs give the impression of being rather "secular," although this term may be too modern to do full justice to the ancient appeal to common sense. It is true that the oldest proverbs show a positive, healthy view toward worldly affairs. Reflecting on various courses of human conduct, the sage suggests that the good life can be won through diligence, sobriety, and prudence, and that the marks of the good life are success, well-being, and a long and fruitful life. In this respect, the proverbs are quite similar to the prudential advice given by sages in Babylonia, Egypt, and elsewhere. Many of the biblical proverbs deal with ordinary problems that hinder a man from attaining fullness of life: laziness (6:6–11; 24:30–34), drunkenness (23:20–21, 29–35), relations with harlots (5:9–10), unwise business dealings (6:1–5), and so on. Judged by the frequency of the nagging-wife theme, the sage seems to have been greatly troubled by this problem:

> A continual dripping on a rainy day,
> and a contentious woman are alike;
> to restrain her is to restrain the wind
> or to grasp oil in his right hand.
> (Prv 27:15–16; cf. 17:1;
> 19:13; 21:9, 19; 25:24)

But beyond all this "secular" advice, there is a tendency to affirm that religious faith is the necessary foundation of the good life. The Deuteronomic historian, it will be recalled, applied the doctrine of rewards and punishments to Israel's history, and tried to show that obedience to Yahweh's Torah insured prosperity and success, whereas disobedience brought hardship and disaster. The wise men of Israel, building on the earlier common-sense view that success is the fruit of prudent living, insisted that the Deuteronomic dogma could be applied to the life of the individual. Thus the way was paved for the identification of Wisdom with Torah in the latest phase of Israel's wisdom literature.

The Fear of the Lord

The characteristic teaching of Israel's sages is summed up at the beginning of the first collection: "The fear of Yahweh is the beginning of knowledge" (1:7; cf. 1:29; 2:5). The same theme is repeated at the conclusion of the collection:

> The fear of Yahweh is the beginning of wisdom,
>   and the knowledge of the Holy One is insight.
>   (Prv 9:10; cf. 15:33;
>   Job 28:28; Ps 111:10)

In this affirmation we have the most direct contact between the wisdom teaching on the one hand, and Israel's prophetic and priestly tradition on the other. According to Israel's sages, wisdom comes not just by observing human conduct or by reflecting on the sayings handed down in the wisdom schools. Rather, true wisdom comes only to the man who acknowledges the sovereignty of Yahweh —who "fears" or reverences the Holy One. Religious faith is the "beginning"—that is, the foundation or the heart—of wisdom. From faith the wise man is led into an understanding of the meaning of life. The "fool," on the other hand, gropes in confusion, regardless of how learned or technically skilled he may be.

You will remember that this same theme had been emphasized by Israel's religious leaders. According to the prophets, "knowledge of God" was the heart of the covenant faith. Hosea, for instance, had insisted that Israel's lack of this knowledge was the fundamental flaw in her history. Similarly, Jeremiah contrasted folly with true wisdom:

> Thus says Yahweh: Let not the wise man glory in his wisdom, let not the mighty man glory in his might, let not the rich man glory in his riches; but let him who glories glory in this, that he understands and knows me, that I am Yahweh who practice kindness, justice, and righteousness in the earth; for in these things I delight, says Yahweh.
>   (Jer 9:23–24)

Yahweh's great acts in history, the prophets insisted, were intended to correct folly and to awaken faith. The New Covenant, according to Jeremiah and Ezekiel, would be a new relationship in which Israel would "know Yahweh." In late Old Testament times, "the fear of the Lord" became a conventional expression for religious faith, and the "God-fearer" was the pious, humble worshiper of God. But in the period of the prophets, "the fear of Yahweh" and "the knowledge of Yahweh" were almost synonymous. Both phrases point to the deepest concern of man's life: his relationship to God.

Wisdom as God's Gift

Thus under the influence of Israel's faith a change took place in the traditional conception of wisdom. In early times, the wise man was regarded as one who had professional skill, owing to his uncanny insight into human affairs (cf. Prv 6:6; 20:18; 21:22; 24:3–6; 30:24–28). Broadly speaking, this skill was regarded as a divine gift. A wise woman, addressing David in extravagant language, could say that "my lord has wisdom like the wisdom of the angel of God to know all things that are on earth" (II Sm 14:20). But in actual practice wisdom meant only extraordinary skill or insight, as in some of the maxims of the book of Proverbs (e.g., 21:22; 24:3–6; 30:24–28). Just as the prophet advanced from the status of a professional seer to that of a religious interpreter of Israel's calling and destiny, however, so the wise man came to be an interpreter of life in its broadest and deepest terms. As the wisdom tradition was adapted to Israel's faith, it yielded a conception of wisdom with which the prophets would have agreed:

> Trust in Yahweh with all your heart,
>   and do not rely on your own insight.
> In all your ways acknowledge him,
>   and he will make straight your paths.
> Be not wise in your own eyes;
>   fear Yahweh, and turn away from evil.
> It will be healing to your flesh,
>   and refreshment to your bones.
>   (Prv 3:5–8)

In a manner reminiscent of Jeremiah (Jer 10:12) or Second Isaiah (Is 40:14, 28), Israel's sages affirmed that wisdom belongs pre-eminently to God.

Yahweh by wisdom founded the earth;
  by understanding he established the heavens;
by his knowledge the deeps broke forth,
  and the clouds drop down the dew.
                                            (Prv 3:19–20)

This wisdom is more than just the key to proper ethical behavior, as in many of the proverbs (e.g., 4:10–19). Rather, it is the key to the divine plan behind the whole creation (30:2–4). That is why the fear of Yahweh is the only beginning of wisdom. Earlier sages had supposed that wisdom helped man to acquire wealth or influence, but later sages affirmed that wisdom far excels the greatest wealth and the most precious treasure. Wisdom comes from God. In exquisite language, the sage portrays Wisdom standing at the gate of the city or in the crowded market place, crying to men to turn aside from folly and follow her footsteps (Prv 1:20–33). Wisdom is God's gift, and blessed is the man who wins it (3:13–20). Indeed, Wisdom is personified as the agent of God's creation (Prv 8–9).

The Wise and the Foolish

Despite all this refinement of the conception of wisdom, the book of Proverbs is governed by a neat doctrine of rewards and punishments. To be sure, the older view that wisdom brings success was superseded by the notion that wisdom itself is the highest good of life. But, according to the sages, this blessing is bestowed upon the good people. The wise are identified with the pious (cf. 9:9; 10:31; 23:24) and are contrasted with the scoffers (9:8, 12; 13:1; 14:6; 15:12; 21:11; 29:8). The Deuteronomic doctrine of the Two Ways (Dt 11:26–28; 30:15–20) was a forceful and urgent appeal for decision in a time of historical crisis; but when it was applied to individuals, as in Proverbs (2:13; 5:5–6; 12:28), it gave rise to certain difficulties. Too easily the sages separated people into two camps—the wise (righteous) and the fools (wicked)—and claimed that rewards and punishments were meted out by Yahweh according to this formula. Psalm 1, which some scholars think was written by a member of the wisdom schools, sets forth the Two Ways. The righteous man is like a tree planted by streams of water; the ungodly man is like the chaff that the wind blows away. The inadequacy of this doctrine was apparent to other wise men, who wrestled more profoundly with the riddle of life's meaning.

VI. LAW

The Word of God

Do you not know, brethren (for I speak to those who know law), that the Law has dominion over a man as long as he lives? For the married woman is bound by the Law while her husband is alive; but if her husband dies, she is set free from the law of the husband. Therefore while her husband is alive, she will be called an adulteress if she be with another man; but if her husband dies, she is set free from the law of the husband, so that she is not an adulteress if she has been with another man. Therefore, my brethren, you also, through the body of Christ, have been made to die to the Law, so as to belong to another who has risen from the dead, in order that we may bring forth fruit unto God. For when we were in the flesh, the sinful passions, which were aroused by the Law, were at work in our members so that they brought forth fruit unto death. But now we have been set free from the Law, having died to that by which we were held down, so that we may serve in a new spirit and not according to the outworn letter.

What shall we say then? Is the Law sin? By no means. Yet I did not know sin save through the Law. For I had not known lust unless the Law had said, "Thou shalt not lust." But sin, having thus found an occasion, worked in me by means of the commandment all manner of lust, for without the Law sin was dead. Once upon a time I was living without law, but when the commandment came, sin revived, and I died, and the commandment that was unto life was discovered in my case to be unto death. For sin, having taken occasion from the commandment, deceived me, and through it killed me. So that the Law indeed is holy and the commandment holy and just and good.

There is therefore now no condemnation for those who are in Christ Jesus, who do not walk according to the flesh. For the law of the Spirit of the life in Christ Jesus has delivered me from the law of sin and of death. For what was impossible to the Law, in that it was weak because of the flesh, God has made good. By sending his Son in the likeness of sinful flesh as a sin-offering, he has condemned sin in the flesh, in order that the requirements of the Law might be fulfilled in us, who walk not according to the flesh but according to the spirit.

(Romans 7:1–12; 8:1–4)

STANISLAS LYONNET, S.J.

St. Paul: Liberty and Law

The favorable reader will find in this fully developed essay a discussion of questions such as these: In what sense is freedom from law a central theme in St. Paul's writing? What is the law from which the Christian is freed, according to St. Paul? Does this freedom extend to the moral content of the Mosaic law? How does comparison with Genesis throw light on St. Paul's teaching on sin and law? What is the difference between sin and transgression? Does St. Paul substitute another law for the one from which the Christian is freed? How are grace and the Holy Spirit related to law? Why does not Christian freedom lead to a breakdown in moral responsibility? If law is not the foundation of Christian morality, what is? Is there room in Christianity for positively formulated rules? What is the difference in Christianity between the written law and the unwritten law? What function do written laws serve for the unjust? For the just? How must external law relate to internal law if it is to be truly Christian? What practical con-

Reproduced with the permission of the Institute of Judaeo-Christian Studies from Volume IV (1962) of its Yearbook, *The Bridge*, edited by John M. Oesterreicher, published by Herder & Herder, New York.

sequences flow from the link in Christianity between love and law? What is the ideal and norm of moral living for a Christian?

Father Stanislas Lyonnet is a professor at the Pontifical Biblical Institute in Rome and the author of many works, especially on the biblical theology of redemption.

St. Paul's assertion admits no compromise: The Christian vocation is a vocation to liberty. The Christian is a son, not a hireling, not a slave. "You have been called to liberty, brethren," he writes to the Galatians. And again: "If you are led by the Spirit, you are not under the Law" (5:13, 18). These proclamations, and others like them, were a source of scandal, not only to the Jews, but even to some of the first Christians. That St. Paul found himself the object of latent hostility, or at least of a painful lack of understanding, from the very beginning of his missionary activity at Antioch about the year 50 until, it would seem, his last days, was mainly, if not solely, due to his attitude toward the Law and to his preaching of Christian liberty.[1] It is this attitude that in our own day continues to alienate those Jews who are sincerely drawn to the person of Christ. True, when circumstances required it, he could make himself all things to all men, even a Jew to the Jews in order to win them (see 1 Cor 9:20)[2] but, as the second chapter of the Epistle to the Galatians indicates, he was unyielding whenever the principle of Christian liberty was at stake. For him it was no secondary doctrine, no side issue; the whole religion of Christ was in the balance.

But it is necessary to understand the precise nature of the liberty he preached. His controversy with the Judaizers, especially in the Epistles to the Galatians and to the Romans, gave him ample opportunity to set forth his ideas as completely as he wished, but his reflections, worked out as they were in very particular historical circumstances, might seem to deal with problems now out of date. Still, I am persuaded that, with a little attention, a doctrine can be extracted from St. Paul's arguments that has undeniable validity and importance for our own day. This doctrine might be summed up in these words: The Christian who is led by the Holy Spirit, and precisely to the extent that he is led by the Spirit, finds himself freed, in Christ, from the Law of Moses; he is freed from it not only as the Law of Moses, but as law. He is delivered from any law that constrains or coerces (I do not say *binds*) him from without;

yet, this in no way makes him an amoral being, outside the realm of good and bad.

Perfectly coherent, this doctrine is, despite appearances, clear and simple as well. It is one that Catholic tradition repeats unceasingly, particularly in the wake of St. Augustine and St. Thomas Aquinas, to mention only those two Doctors of the Church. If this doctrine of freedom always seems new to us, it is because in everyday life we are apt to forget it.

Deliverance from Law

When he speaks of law, St. Paul obviously has in mind, above all, that Law which for him and for his Jewish contemporaries was uniquely worthy of the title, the legislation given on Mount Sinai. To measure the offense his statements must needs have given to his fellow Jews, we only have to recall the veneration, the honor, with which they surrounded the Torah. Having in their minds become identified with the divine wisdom, the Law itself could proclaim:

> "Before all ages, in the beginning, he created me,
>   and through all ages I shall not cease to be. . . .
> Come to me, all you that yearn for me,
>   and be filled with my fruits. . . .
> He who eats of me will hunger still,
>   he who drinks of me will thirst for more;
> He who obeys me will not be put to shame,
>   he who serves me will never fail."
> All this is true of the book of the Most High's covenant,
>   the Law which Moses commanded us. . . .
>   (Ecclus 24:9, 18, 20–22)

The Law was the word of God, the water that slakes all thirst, the life-giving bread, the vine laden with delectable fruit; in it were hidden the treasures of wisdom and knowledge. In short, the Law held the place St. John and St. Paul were rightly to announce as that of the Christ.[3]

But from this Law the Christian has been delivered, St. Paul unequivocally declares: "You are not under the Law but under grace" (Rom 6:14). A wife is bound to her husband as long as he is alive, but, when he dies, is completely free from the law that bound her to him, so that she is not an adulteress if she marries another. In like manner the Christian, united to Christ dead and risen, is dead to the

Law, delivered from it, no longer its subject (see Rom 7:1-6). But had the Law no role to play in the history of the chosen people? Indeed, but it was the thankless one of a jailer, or of a pedagogue, the slave whose task it was, not to teach the children, but to lead them to their teacher (see Gal 3:23-24). Beyond this, St. Paul paradoxically asserts that the Law, which the Jews revere as the source of life, has been imposed by God on man to bring him death. The economy of the Law was not that of a blessing but of a curse (see Gal 3:10).

"What then was the Law?" he asks in the Epistle to the Galatians (3:19), and his answer is that it was given to make room for transgression. This was a shocking statement, even for Christian readers, and well-meaning copyists very soon tried to soften its harshness.[4] In spite of the context, many ancient commentators, both Greek and Latin, interpreted the Apostle as saying that the Law had been enacted to repress, reduce, or curb transgressions, but this is an impossible subterfuge.[5] The text is concerned with provoking transgressions, not with repressing them.

Is this an extravagance? Is it a paradox? Not at all! It is true that the Epistle to the Romans offers a more carefully worked out argument (see Rom 5:20-21; 7:5-23). There the Apostle's thought acquires a richness and balance that the impassioned, polemic tones of his earlier Letter to the Galatians prevented him from reaching. His teaching, however, remains unchanged. What is more, the dialectic of Romans brings out St. Paul's idea with even greater precision. Emancipation from the Law is one of the essential links, indeed, the final one, of his argument. Freed from sin, from death, and from the flesh, the Christian cannot be saved unless he is also freed from the Law; only this final liberation will dispossess sin of its power, its dominion over man: "Sin shall not have dominion over you, since you are not under the Law, but under grace" (Rom 6:14). To be under the Law, then, is the same as to be under the dominion of sin: never before had St. Paul been so incisive.

A source of scandal for the Jews, such assertions in turn run the opposite risk of leaving the modern Christian reader quite indifferent. He has never felt any strong attachment for the Law of Moses; he finds it quite normal not to be obliged to observe its complicated ritual or its profusion of observances—as circumcision, the minute prescriptions for keeping the Sabbath, for preparing food, or for contacts with the pagan world—which, as far as he can see, have no real religious value. As a matter of fact, had St. Paul intended no more than the Christian's deliverance from these obligations, his statements would hardly raise problems. Nor would they offer any great interest for the man of today. But so understood, they would be a caricature of his true teaching. Granting that such an interpretation has been seriously defended,[6] the context of the Epistle to the Romans, if not that to the Galatians, is so clearly opposed to it that no exegete dreams of proposing it.

Under the term "law," St. Paul certainly includes that part of the Mosaic legislation which concerns the moral life in its strict sense; in fact, the Epistle to the Romans speaks of no other aspect of the Law but the moral one. As for the seventh chapter, where the question is expressly treated, everyone must at least see with Father Huby that, if St. Paul has the Law of Moses in mind, it is "not in its ritual and ceremonial positions" that he considers it, "but in its permanent moral content." [7] In other words, he is concerned with the Law of Moses as a positive expression of the natural law. Besides, St. Paul is explicit. The "law of sin and of death" [8]—that is, the Law that provokes sin and leads to death—from which, he proclaims, we are free (see 8:2) is clearly designated by means of one of the precepts of the Decalogue: "I did not know sin save through the Law. For I had not known lust unless the Law had said: 'Thou shalt not lust'" (7:7).

Let us press this passage further. The English and Latin translations, "Thou shalt not lust," *Non concupisces,* may suggest that the Apostle has a particular commandment in mind, the one that prohibits carnal desires. This would be a serious mistake. Not only is the context of Exodus 20:17 or of Deuteronomy 5:21, from which this prohibition is taken, utterly opposed to such an interpretation, but in the Septuagint, the Greek word *epithumein,* whether in its verbal or substantive form, hardly ever evokes the idea of carnal desire. What the commandment forbids, in the most general sense, is the craving for what belongs to another, whether it be his house, his wife, his slave, his ox or ass, or anything else that he owns.[9] In much the same way, Ecclesiasticus sums up the whole Jewish Law in the one precept: "Avoid all evil" (17:12). For Ben Sirach, this precept seems to epitomize not only the legislation of Sinai but all the expressions of God's will that have been given to man since his creation, expressions that have their synthesis in a unique law and covenant.[10]

It is not surprising, then, that St. Paul in turn should choose an all-embracing formula, one that could be applied to every divine command and, indeed, contains them all, even the prohibition imposed upon our first parents, the prototype of all others. In his desire to describe how man becomes conscious of sin, to describe, too, the essential role played by law in this process, he spontaneously thinks of the biblical description of the sin that became the pattern of all our sins; all succeeding generations of men unfailingly share in it and reproduce it again and again in their own lives.[11] Many have noticed that more than one detail in this seventh chapter of Romans is in some way reminiscent of the third chapter of Genesis.[12] In any case, keeping in mind the narrative of Genesis may help throw light on a passage that is at first sight enigmatic, and suddenly clarify it.

Adam and Eve are living in a state of familiarity with God, when the serpent comes upon the scene and succeeds in persuading them that they will be like gods if they taste of the tree of the knowledge of good and evil. Suddenly, the fruit, which has become the means of securing this divine privilege, seems to Eve's eyes an unknown delight. The Bible brings this out emphatically: "The woman saw that the tree was good for food, pleasing to the eyes, and desirable for the knowledge it would give" (Gn 3:6).[13] But hardly have they violated God's command, when they find themselves reduced to nakedness, stripped of everything that previously constituted their happiness; once, they were God's friends, but now they hide from him, fear him, and flee from him. They have been forever driven from the garden, that is, from intimacy with God, and the cherubim with the flaming sword henceforth forbid them and their descendants to enter. Unless God himself mercifully intervenes, the way that leads to the tree of life—of that life which belongs to God alone, and to those who are united to him—is forever shut. Now God's command was unquestionably good, spiritual, divine. It is not the command but the serpent who is responsible for all the world's ills. And yet, according to the biblical account, the command did play a role; the serpent used it to induce our first parents to disobedience. Though it was intended to preserve life in them, in reality it became a cause or, at least, an occasion of death.

Such, I think, is the precise point St. Paul is trying to make in the much discussed passage of his Epistle to the Romans. There is only one change in the cast of characters: Sin, personified, plays the part of the serpent.[14]

"What shall we say then? Is the Law sin? By no means! Yet I did not know sin save through the Law. For I had not known [15] lust unless the Law had said: 'Thou shalt not lust!' But sin, having thus found an occasion, worked in me by means of the commandment all manner of lust, for without the Law, sin was dead" (Rom 7:7-8). It was dead like a dormant snake, Father Huby comments almost in spite of himself, so strongly does the Genesis account impose itself upon his mind.[16] Even more in accordance with St. Paul's text, sin was dead as is *nekros,* a powerless corpse. St. Paul continues: "Once upon a time I was living without law" (7:9). This was truer of Adam than of any other man, of Adam and Eve before the sin-serpent wormed itself into them, as it were, creating in them that partnership of guilt which consisted in their desire to be like gods, a desire embodied in their longing for a taste of the forbidden tree.

Making the necessary allowances, these words of St. Paul could be applied to any circumcised Jew or baptized Christian, and in a certain sense to every human being, insofar as he has not yet, by a first free act, ordered his being to its last end.[17] "But," the Apostle continues, "when the commandment came, sin revived, *anezēsen";* heretofore a lifeless body, *nekros,* it rose up, *ana,* a living thing, *ezēsen,* "and I died," that is, I lost that eminently divine privilege of life. "And the commandment that was unto life was discovered in my case to be unto death. For sin having taken occasion from the commandment, deceived me"—as the serpent deceived Eve [18]—"and through it killed me" (Rom 7:9-11). For St. Paul, then, just as for the authors of Genesis 3 and Wisdom 2:24, the one responsible for death is neither the Law nor its Author, but the serpent or the devil or sin. The conclusion is obvious: "The Law indeed is holy and the commandment holy and just and good" (7:12).

How are we then to explain God's strange conduct? If he desires nothing but life, why give man a law that, in fact, will lead him to death? Having asked this question, St. Paul immediately provides the answer: "Did then that which is good become death to me? By no means! But sin, that it might be manifest as sin, worked death for me through that which is good, in order that sin by reason of the commandment might become immeasurably sinful" (7:13), in other words, that sin might exercise its full power as sin by means of the commandment.

The decisive word has been spoken. According to the Jews, the Law conferred life, but a law as such, even if it proposed the most sublime ideal, could not transform a creature of flesh into a spiritual being, alive with the very life of God. If this were possible, it would mean that man has no need of being saved, that he can actually save himself! Far from conferring life, far from destroying or even repressing and curbing the death-bearing power of sin in man, the purpose of the Law is, as it were, to permit sin to exercise all its virulence but, in so doing, to bring itself out into the open and unmask itself. The Law does not take sin away, rather does it reveal to man his sinful state.[19] Thus in the garden, when the serpent induced the woman, who looked upon him as a sincere friend and counselor, to violate the divine command, he showed his true colors: the most dangerous of enemies, the supreme sinner—a liar and a murderer, St. John calls him (see 8:44)—one who had turned from God, he now turns others from him who is life.

Let us note in the margin that, properly speaking, law does not provoke sin, but transgression. Undoubtedly, we are accustomed to identifying the two concepts and to defining sin as a violation of a divine law, in order to accentuate its religious aspect, upon which the Bible is so insistent. St. Paul, more than anyone else, considers sin an opposition to God, but usually takes care not to confuse it with simple transgression. In this, he is faithful to the teaching of Genesis which places the sin of Adam and Eve not so much in the act of disobedience to God's command, but beyond it, in their desire to be like God. Thus the serpent, without having transgressed any formal precept, nevertheless sinned the most grievously; of the three personalities portrayed, he is the most severely punished and the only one cursed.

St. Paul looks upon transgression as the expression, the exteriorization, of a much more radical evil, *hamartia*: an evil power personified, which is often reduced to mere carnal concupiscence, but which in reality more nearly corresponds to that deeply rooted egoism by which man, since original sin, orders everything to himself instead of ordering himself to God and to others. St. Augustine calls it self-love, architect of the City of Evil, and St. Paul plainly, "hostility to God" (Rom 8:7).[20] It is this "sin" that must be destroyed in us, and left to itself law is incapable of the task. But by permitting "transgression," law enables sin to reveal its true identity and man, schooled by his painful experience, to have recourse to the one Savior. This is the way St. Paul understands the role of law, a role indispensable, ultimately beneficent and salutary. But this role is not the privilege of a particular code, not even that of Moses; rather does it fall to any law that is truly law, to any norm that is imposed on man's conscience from without. Consequently, it is from the "rule of law" as such that St. Paul declares the Christian freed.

The Law of the Spirit

Is the Christian, then, a man without law, a creature beyond the realm of good and evil? St. Paul clearly foresaw this objection and his answer was a flat denial of its validity: "What then? Are we to sin because we are not under the Law but under grace? By no means!" (Rom 6:15). Indeed, nothing could more openly contradict the teaching of all his epistles, and if it seemed logical to draw such a conclusion from the premises I have established, then I should certainly have erred in the course of establishing them. Now, this apparent conflict must be resolved. The eighth chapter of the Epistle to the Romans, taking up again the line of thought that had been sketched out in the Letter to the Galatians, furnishes, I believe, all the elements of a solution. The most authoritative interpreters of Catholic tradition, in the face of this difficulty, have been content to repeat St. Paul's statements without attemping to mitigate them. In a matter so delicate, I shall be allowed to refer to these authorities, particularly to St. Thomas, who, in his commentary on the Epistles of St. Paul, recorded the ultimate expression of his thought.[21]

Chapters 5, 6, and 7 of the Epistle to the Romans have set forth the conditions necessary for the Christian to be saved: deliverance from sin, from death, from the flesh, and the final but no less indispensable deliverance, that from the Law. They demonstrate that each successive deliverance is acquired for the Christian in Christ, and in him alone. Hence, chapter 8 can begin with a cry of triumph: "There is therefore now no condemnation for those who are in Christ Jesus!" St. Paul states the reason precisely: "For the law of the Spirit, [giving] life in Christ Jesus, has delivered me from the law of sin and of death" (8:1–2). Thus man is delivered from that Law which, according to the incontestable testimony of the Bible, had been the instrument of sin and death, by something that St. Paul (surprisingly, to say the least) also calls a law: the law of the life-giving Spirit. What does this mean? Can Christ have been satisfied with substituting for the Law of Moses another code, more perfect or less complicated perhaps, but of the same nature, which would therefore keep the Christian under legal rule? This would contradict all that has gone before. Only a moment ago, St. Paul had opposed to the Law of Moses not another law, but grace: if sin no longer exercises its dominion over you, he explains, it is because "you are not under the Law but under grace" (Rom 6:14). Has he changed his mind? Not at all! His choice of expression has changed, but not his thinking.

Tradition, furthermore, has not failed to grasp his line of thought. St. Thomas, for example, sums it all up so clearly and succinctly that there is no room for ambiguity: "The law of the Spirit," he writes in his commentary on Romans 8, "is what we call the New Law" —an observation to be kept in mind if we are to understand properly those passages of the *Summa Theologica* and the *Summa Contra Gentiles* in which the Angelic Doctor expounds the "New Law" as a theologian. He continues: "Now the law of the Spirit is identified either with the person of the Holy Spirit or with the activity of that same Spirit in us." Lest anyone misunderstand the meaning he intends to convey by these words, he adds a comparison with the Old Law, recalling that just previously "the Apostle said of it that it was spiritual." [22] It is spiritual, St. Thomas explains, in the sense that it is "given by the Holy Spirit."

The "law of the Spirit," then, does not differ from the Law of Moses—and a fortiori from all nonrevealed law, even if looked upon as the expression of the divine will—merely because it proposes a loftier ideal and imposes greater demands. Nor does it differ because it offers salvation at a bargain, as if Christ had replaced the unbearable yoke of the Law of Sinai with an "easy morality," which would be a scandal, indeed. No, the law of the Spirit is radically different by its very nature. It is not just a code, not even one "given by the Holy Spirit," but a law "produced in us by the Holy Spirit"; not a simple norm of actions outside us, but something that no legal code as such can possibly be: a new, inner, source of spiritual energy.

If St. Paul applies the term "law" to this spiritual energy, rather than the term "grace" that he uses elsewhere (see Rom 6:14), he most probably does it because of Jeremiah's prophecy (also mentioned in this context by St. Thomas) announcing a new covenant, the "New Testament." For the prophet, too, speaks of law: "This is the covenant which I will make with the house of Israel. . . . I will

place my law within them, and write it upon their hearts" (31:33).
Every time the Angelic Doctor refers to this "New Testament," he
does so in the same terms: "It is God's way to act in the interior
of the soul, and it was thus that the New Testament was given,
since it consists in the inpouring of the Holy Spirit." Again: "It is
the Holy Spirit himself who is the New Testament, inasmuch as he
works in us the love that is the fullness of the Law." [23] For the
Church and for her liturgy, too, the promulgation of the New Law
does not date from the Sermon on the Mount, but from the day of
Pentecost when the "finger of the Father's right hand," *digitus
paternae dexterae*, wrote his law in the hearts of men; the code of
the Old Law given on Sinai finds its counterpart, not in a new code,
but in the giving of the Holy Spirit.[24] In the beautiful words of
Cardinal Seripando, it is this Spirit that the Christian "receives to
take the Law's place." [25]

No need, therefore, to fear a breakdown of moral responsibility.
The Christian who receives the Holy Spirit as an active force within
him or, in words that mean the same, who receives this activity of
the Spirit, becomes capable of "walking according to the Spirit," that
is, walking in conformity with what the Old Law, "spiritual" though
it was, demanded of him in vain. This is why St. Paul, after pro-
claiming man's deliverance by the law of the Spirit, thanks to the
redemptive work of Christ, can attribute to that work the following
aim: "in order that the justification of the Law"—that justification
which the Law wished but could not obtain from the creatures of
flesh that we were—"might be fulfilled in us" (Rom 8:4). Mark the
nuance of fullness suggested by the verb "fulfill," as when a prophecy is fulfilled in its accomplishment, or a type in its antitype.[26]
"Fulfill" here is in the passive, so conscious is St. Paul that this "fulfillment," while remaining a free act of man, is even more truly an
act of God, an act of the Spirit who is at work in man.

From this fundamental doctrine everything else flows, notably the
fact that Christian morality is of necessity founded on love, as St.
Paul, following his Master, teaches: "The whole Law is fulfilled in
one word: Thou shalt love thy neighbor as thyself" (Gal 5:14). "He
who loves his neighbor has fulfilled the Law. . . . If there is any
other commandment, it is summed up in this saying: Thou shalt love
thy neighbor as thyself. . . . Love therefore is the fulfillment of the
Law" (Rom 13:8–10). The reason is that love is not first of all a

norm of conduct, but a dynamic force. As St. Thomas notes, it is precisely because the Law, as a law, was not love that it could not justify man: "Consequently it was necessary to give us a law of the Spirit, who by producing love within us, could give us life." [27]

Under these conditions, it is easy to see that a Christian, that is, a man led by the Holy Spirit,[28] can at the same time be freed from every external law—"not be under the Law"—and yet lead a perfect moral and virtuous life. St. Paul makes this abundantly clear in the Epistle to the Galatians, shortly after he has reduced the whole Law to love: "Walk in the Spirit, and you will not fulfill the lusts of the flesh" (Gal 5:16). Nothing could be more obvious, he explains, since these are two antagonistic principles: if you follow one, you cannot but oppose the other. "If you are led by the Spirit, you are not under the Law." In fact, what need would you have of law? A spiritual man knows perfectly well what is carnal and, if he is spiritual, he will fly from it as by instinct, fly from "immorality, uncleanness, licentiousness, idolatry, witchcrafts, enmities, contentions, jealousies, anger, quarrels, factions, parties, envies, murders, drunkenness, carousings, and suchlike" (5:19–21).

To be guilty of such misdeeds would clearly indicate that one is not led by the Spirit. "Concerning these things I warn you, as I have warned you, that they who do such things will not attain the kingdom of God" (5:21). But these misdeeds you will not commit once you are spiritual. The fruits you will produce then will be those of the Spirit. Perhaps it would be better to say "the fruit," since there is really only one with many facets: "Charity, joy, peace, patience, kindness, goodness, faith, modesty, continency" (5:22), in brief, the whole procession of Christian virtues. For St. Paul they are nothing but so many expressions of charity:

> Charity is patient, is kind; charity does not envy, is not pretentious, is not puffed up, is not ambitious, is not self-seeking, is not provoked; thinks no evil, does not rejoice over wickedness, but rejoices with the truth; bears with all things, believes all things, hopes all things, endures all things.
>
> (1 Cor 13:4–7)

Since he has no need, then, for a law to constrain him from without, the Christian, led by the Spirit, fulfills every law in the full liberty of the sons of God.

In the light of these explanations, it is surprising that Father Prat should find it "difficult to see [in St. Paul] a governing principle of moral teaching," or that he could have written this astonishing passage:

> That is precisely the delicate—I was about to say the weak—point of Paul's moral teaching: After having completely done away with the Mosaic Law, he never says clearly with what he replaces it. . . . In seeing Paul intent on destroying the whole edifice of the ancient Law, without appearing to think of reconstructing it, we ask with anxiety where this work of demolition is going to stop, and on what foundation the obligation of the new dispensation is to rest.[29]

The Code of Christian Laws

More than one reader will share Father Prat's perplexity, and his dilemma is not imaginary. There is no question but that the Christian religion involves certain positive laws. St. Paul himself does not hesitate to promulgate some, and they are often of a very precise nature. The morality of the New Testament, including that of the Apostle, has nothing in common with a "morality without obligation or sanction." [30] Upon the catechumen who asks for baptism the Church, in this resembling the Synagogue, fully intends to impose a code of morality that, though less complicated and more sublime, is nonetheless a code of laws. Besides, when we speak of the New Law as opposed to the Old, is it not of this aspect that we ordinarily think before and above all others?

Ordinarily perhaps; and, undoubtedly, it is this aspect that was in Father Prat's mind. But it was not, I think, in St. Paul's. True, on two different occasions he does speak of the "law of Christ" (Gal 6:2; 1 Cor 9:21),[31] but what he opposes to the Old Law is grace or the law of the Spirit which, as we have seen, comes to the same thing. Nor is this the approach of St. Thomas, who was certainly familiar with the classic opposition between the Old Law and the New. When seeking to define the latter, he is careful not to designate it primarily as a code of laws: "That which is preponderant [in it] is the grace of the Holy Ghost, which is given through faith in Christ. Consequently the New Law is chiefly the grace itself of the Holy Ghost, which is given to those who believe in Christ." [32] It is an unwritten law, he adds, and hence able to justify man. But to the extent that it is a code of written laws, to the extent that it contains the teachings of faith and moral precepts that govern human attitudes and acts, the New Law does not justify any more than did the Old Law since its nature is not different: it remains a norm of conduct, not a principle of activity. Thus, commenting on the Apostle's say-

ing, "the letter kills" (2 Cor 3:6), the Angelic Doctor, in the steps of
St. Augustine,[33] does not for a moment hesitate to write: "The letter
denotes any writing that is external to man, even that of the moral
precepts such as are contained in the Gospel. Wherefore the letter,
even of the Gospel, would kill, unless there were the inward presence of the healing grace of faith." [34]

Even after the Protestant controversies the language remains unchanged. There is, for example, St. Robert Bellarmine, whose comment on the Pauline opposition between the "law of works" and the
"law of faith" (see Rom 3:27) [35] is no less faithful to St. Augustine's
De Spiritu et Littera:

> The law of faith is faith itself, which obtains the grace for action,
> whereas the law of works is satisfied with commanding the same.
>
> The law of works is the letter which kills, and the law of faith is the
> Spirit who gives life.
>
> From this it follows that not only the law of Moses, but even the
> law of Christ, to the extent that it commands something, is the law of
> works, whereas the law of faith is the spirit of faith, by which not only
> we who are Christians, but the patriarchs as well, and the prophets,
> and all just men, have obtained the free gift of God's grace, and, once
> justified by that grace, have kept the commandments of the law.[36]

Why, then, does the religion of Christ still require a code of laws?
Why should there be kept, alongside the chief, unwritten element
that justifies, another, written element that does not justify? If this
state of affairs was strange in the old economy, does it not become
incomprehensible in the economy of grace? Not at all!

The Pauline principle most certainly remains: "The Law is not
made for the just, but for the unjust" (1 Tim 1:9). If all Christians
were just, there would be no need to restrain them by laws. Law, as
a rule, does not enter upon the scene except to repress an existing
disorder. For example, as long as Christians received Communion
frequently, the Church never thought of obligating them under pain
of mortal sin to do so at least once a year.[37] But when fervor de-
clined, she promulgated the precept of Easter Communion, in order
to remind her faithful that it is impossible to possess divine life
without being nourished by the flesh of the Christ. Even though all
are subject to this law, it is really not directed to the fervent Christian who continues to receive Communion during the paschal season
not, as St. Thomas puts it, because of the Lord's command, but because of that inner need which prompts him to communicate every
Sunday or even every day of the year.[38] This does not imply that he

is no longer bound by the precept but that, as long as he experiences this inner need—which is a fruit of the Holy Spirit leading him—he will in fact fulfill [39] the precept superabundantly, without even adverting to the fact. On the other hand, as soon as that inner need no longer makes itself felt, the law is there to constrain him and to warn him that he is no longer being led by the Spirit.

In such a case this law will play the same role for the Christian that the Law of Moses did for the Jew.[40] As a pedagogue to lead him to the Christ, it will not only act as a sort of substitute for the light no longer supplied by the Holy Spirit, but will, above all, help him to recognize his condition as a sinner—a condition which is by definition that of one who is no longer led by the Holy Spirit. And since, as we have seen, such a recognition is in St. Paul's judgment the first requirement for man's cure, it becomes evident that the law was made for sinners.

But the law is not without utility even for the just. Although he is in the state of grace, that is, led by the Holy Spirit, the Christian, as long as he remains on earth, possesses the Spirit only imperfectly, as a sort of pledge (see Rom 8:23; 2 Cor 1:22). As long as he lives in a mortal body, he is never so completely freed from sin and from the flesh that he cannot at any moment fall back under their domination. Now in this unstable situation, the external, the written law, objective norm of man's moral conduct, will help his conscience which is so easily clouded by his passions—for the flesh continues to struggle against the spirit (see Gal 5:17)—to distinguish unerringly the works of the flesh from the fruit of the Spirit, and not to confuse the inclinations of his own sin-wounded nature with the inner promptings of the Spirit. St. Paul does not consider it superfluous to remind his readers what it is that the Spirit suggests to the genuinely spiritual man, nor to add to his doctrinal discussions exhortations meant to govern their moral life. Until the Christian acquires full spiritualization in heaven, his liberty will remain imperfect, inchoative; [41] alongside the chief element of spiritualization, grace, alone able to justify, there will be a secondary element, no more able to justify than was the Old Law, but still indispensable for sinners, and by no means superfluous for the imperfectly just that we all are.[42]

Still, it is necessary that this secondary element remain secondary, and that it not imperceptibly tend to assume the role of the principal element, which is what happened to the Jewish Law in St. Paul's time. To ward off this ever-threatening danger, it is well to recall a basic principle which is only a corollary of the doctrine I have been setting forth till now, and which St. Thomas has succeeded in stating with his usual clarity: The external law may only be the expression of the interior law.

In his treatise on law in the *Summa Theologica*, St. Thomas asks if the New Law should command or prohibit external works, that is, if it should involve a code of positive laws. His reply begins by reaffirming the doctrine that the preponderant part of the New Law is the inner grace of the Holy Spirit. Works can be commanded only in virtue of a necessary relation to that inner grace. Either they will be works that put us in contact with the humanity of the Christ, from whom flows all grace, and are therefore necessary to produce in us the inner dynamism that is faith working through charity. Or they will be works that translate and give concrete expression to this inner dynamism. If works possess a necessary relationship to this inner energy, they are commanded or forbidden in the code of the New Law. If, on the other hand, they have no essential connection with the interior law, they are neither commanded nor forbidden in the New Law Christ and the apostles promulgated. They are left to the discretion of the legislator who can command or forbid them in every case in which concrete circumstances indicate that for a certain group of Christians, or for the whole Church, there exists a necessary connection with the interior law of love—in other words, whenever such works become in practice the necessary expression of that law.[43]

One consequence of this link between love and law is that, for the Christian, any purely external violation of law, a violation that by definition is unrelated to the interior law, cannot be a genuine violation. The notion of "involuntary sin" which occupies so large a place in the Mosaic legislation—the sin-offerings of Leviticus were meant to expiate precisely offenses of that kind—carries no meaning for the Christian. Of course, a purely material sin can have tragic consequences, either because of the habits to which it gives rise or because of its social repercussions but it is not a fault, in the strict sense of the word, requiring forgiveness.

On the other hand, an observance devoid of love is also devoid of meaning. Anyone who attaches an independent value to mere observance will try to keep it up at any cost; he may even imagine that he is still obeying the law when he is in fact dodging or circum-venting or "outwitting" it.[44] For the man who sees in the outward observance nothing but an expression of the inner law, such an attitude is unthinkable. Since the sole aim of external law is to safe-guard the Christian's inner dynamism, it derives all its value from the latter, not the other way around. What is essential, then, is not the observance of this or that practice of penance but the spirit of penance, not this or that pious practice but the spirit of prayer, for the practice is required only for the purpose of preserving the spirit. Without neglecting the latter, the Christian is above all concerned with the spirit; he does not think that he can truly observe a law until he has fully grasped its significance, that is, until he has pondered the conditions under which a law will make concrete the inner prompting he does—or should—experience.[45]

Another consequence of the relationship between love and law is that ordinarily the outward law will not provide the Christian with an ideal, the attainment of which could possibly satisfy him, but simply with a minimum below which the dynamism that constitutes him as a Christian will inevitably fail him. It is for this reason that the code of the New Law, while including a series of positive pre-scriptions and prohibitions, before all else offers the Christian a norm of a completely different nature: the imitation of the person of the Christ, particularly of his love, which in turn is a reflection of the love of the Father. This is an objective norm, for Christ is not the creation of man's imagination, but a historical personality whose life and deeds have been recorded for us in the Gospels.[46] In fact, St. Paul hardly knows another norm; following the example of Christ, who commanded his disciples to be perfect as their heavenly Father is perfect, St. Paul can only repeat to his faithful that they should contemplate Christ and imitate him:

> Be kind to one another, and merciful, generously forgiving one an-other, as also God in Christ has generously forgiven you. Be you, there-fore, imitators of God, as very dear children and walk in love, as Christ also loved us and delivered himself up for us.
>
> (Eph 4:32–5:2)

And the whole morality of marriage is summed up in one command:

> Just as the Church is subject to Christ, so also let wives be subject to their husbands in all things. Husbands, love your wives, just as Christ also loved the Church, and delivered himself up for her, that he might sanctify her.
>
> (Eph 5:24–26)

The pious Jew, so zealous in his devotion to the Law, strove to know it better and better, so that he might observe its most minute details. The manual of the Qumran community provides that whenever there are found ten members, "let there be among them a man who studies the Law day and night, continually, for the improvement of all." [47] For a Christian, it is the person of the Christ who is the whole law, not only with regard to its principal element, the spirit of Christ imparted to him, but even with regard to its secondary element, which, in the magnificent words of Father de Foucauld, is finally brought back to the imitation of Christ: "Your rule? To follow me. Do what I would do. In everything, ask yourself what would our Lord have done. And do it. This is your only rule, but it is your absolute rule." [48]

A final consequence: When a Christian acts in this way, he is free, for "where the Spirit of the Lord is, there is freedom" (2 Cor 3:17). This is a theme dear to St. Augustine, but not less so to St. Thomas who writes:

> A man who acts of his own accord, acts freely, but one who is impelled by another, is not free. He who avoids evil, not because it is evil, but because a precept of the Lord forbids it, is not free. On the other hand, he who avoids evil because it is evil, is free. [49] Now it is precisely this the Holy Spirit accomplishes, by inwardly equipping the soul with an inner dynamism. The result is that a man refrains from evil out of love, as though the divine law were commanding him, and thus he is free, not because he is not subject to the divine law, but because his inner dynamism makes him do what the divine law requires. [50]

In the *Summa Contra Gentiles*, when referring to the same Pauline adage on freedom, St. Thomas does not modify his language. [51] Silvester of Ferrara, too, comments:

> The just are under the divine law, which binds them without constraining them, to the extent that they observe the precepts of the law in a fully free and voluntary manner, not constrained by fear of punishment or the order of a superior, as are the wicked, who would not observe what the law requires were there no divine command and did they not fear being punished for their transgression. [52]

References

1 Among the many indications of this opposition to be found in St. Paul's letters, there is the moving plea of Phil 1:15–17, and the anxiety that beset the Apostle as he was about to hand over to the mother church on Jerusalem the collection he had so tirelessly gathered among the churches of the diaspora (see Rom 15:25–31).

[2] There is no reason, therefore, to doubt the account of Timothy's circumcision (see Ac 16:3) nor that of St. Paul's compliance in Jerusalem with the wishes of St. James (see 21:24).

[3] This theme is found throughout St. John's Gospel, also in Col 2:3. Father Joseph Bonsirven, S.J., aptly remarks that a Christian reading the writings of the rabbis gains the impression that the Law is to them what Christ is to him. (See "Judaïsme Palestinien au temps de Jésus Christ," *Dictionnaire de la bible, Supplément,* IV, 1185).

[4] The Chester Beatty Papyrus, oldest witness of the direct tradition, has a text from which the word "transgression" has disappeared: "Why then the law of works until the offspring should come . . . ?" Others interpret this sentence differently: "Why then the law of works? It was enacted until the offspring should come. . . ."

[5] Among the ancient commentators are such outstanding ones as St. Chrysostom, Theodoret, St. Jerome, and Pelagius.

[6] Occasionally, an interpretation of this kind is implied in formulas that are ambiguous; for example, that St. Paul rejects the Old Law *in its positive aspects,* but not the moral law as founded on man's nature. We shall see that, in a certain sense, this is quite correct; but the Law of Moses made no such distinction, and neither did St. Paul.

[7] Joseph Huby, S.J., *Saint Paul épître aux romains* (Paris: Beauchesne, 1957), p. 234. "No allusion is made either to circumcision or to the other rites of Judaism" (*ibid.,* p. 231).

[8] See Rom 8:2: "The law of the Spirit [giving] life in Christ Jesus has delivered me from the law of sin and of death."

[9] "You shall not covet, *epithumein* (Hebrew: ḥmd), your neighbor's house. You shall not covet your neighbor's wife, nor his male or female slave, nor his ox or ass, nor anything else that belongs to him" (Ex 20:17). Again: "You shall not covet, *epithumein* (ḥmd), your neighbor's wife. You shall not desire, *epithumein* ('wh), your neighbor's house or field, nor his male or female slave, nor his ox or ass, nor anything that belongs to him" (Dt 5:21). Likewise, the place named *Kibrot-hattaavah,* the Graves of Greed, *epithumia* ('wh), recalls the episode of the quail and the divine punishment inflicted upon "the greedy, *epithumētēs* ('wh) people" (see Nm 11:34; 33:17).

[10] Some commentators distinguish between two sections in this passage of Ben Sirach. The first (see 17:1–8) treats of creation, while in the second (see 17:9–11) "the author apparently passes from man in general to the Hebrew people in particular." (These words are those of Joseph Bonsirven, S.J., in his edition of *La Sainte Bible du Chanoine Crampon* [Paris: Desclée, 1952].) To judge by his wording, Father Bonsirven does not seem to adopt this particular point of view. In any case, the transition is imperceptible. Verse 9, while certainly referring to the Law of Moses, probably alludes (as Dom Calmet noted long ago) to the two trees in the garden of Eden: "He has set before them *knowledge,* a law of *life* as their inheritance." On the other hand, verse 6, recalling the precept given to Adam, says: "Good and evil he shows them"—a phrasing that practically reproduces the words of Moses when summing up the Law of Sinai: "I have set before you life and death, the good and the evil" (Dt 30:15, 19, according to the Septuagint). Cf. Huby, *op. cit.,* p. 600.

[11] See Rom 5:12, and this writer's notes in the *Bible de Jérusalem.* (A brief English résumé of Father Lyonnet's interpretation of this much discussed verse can be found in "Original Sin and Romans 5:12–14," *Theology Digest,* 5, 1 (Winter 1957), 54–57 [Translator].) In the seventh chapter of Romans, it is not St. Paul's aim to describe the sin of Adam for its own sake; he is not writing as a historian, but as a theologian. His source of information, however, is

not psychological introspection, as many have supposed, but the Old Testament.

12 So Methodius of Olympia (see *De Resurrectione* II, 1–8), Theodore of Mopsuestia, Severian of Gabala, Theodoret, and Gennadius of Constantinople, among the early writers; Cajetan, in the sixteenth century, and Lietzmann, Lagrange, and many others, among the moderns. Even among those who reject this interpretation, a good number concede that St. Paul took the Genesis account as his model. In his recent commentary, F. J. Leenhardt, too, writes that the affinity between verses 7–12 and Genesis 3 shows that the Apostle built his scenery with Adam in the background. See *L'épître de Saint Paul aux Romains* (Neuchâtel, 1957), p. 100. See also Peter Bläser, *Das Gesetz bei Paulus* (Münster: Aschendorff, 1941), p. 115, n. 77, and A. Feuillet who speaks of "features obviously borrowed from the scene of Adam's and Eve's disobedience in paradise, a fault which in some way was the prototype of all that followed" (*Lumière et Vie*, 14 [1954], 222). Cf. Huby, *op. cit.*, pp. 601–4.

13 The Hebrew terms translated here by "pleasing" and "desirable" (*'wh* and *hmd*) are the same one finds in the expression "graves of greed or craving" and in the prohibition of the Decalogue: "Thou shalt not covet, not lust." (See above, n. 9.)

14 Diodorus of Tarsus said as much when he wrote: "He seems to call the devil sin." (*Pauluskommentare aus der Griechischen Kirche*, ed. Karl Staab [Münster: Aschendorff, 1932], p. 87.) One might compare Rom 5:12: "Through one man sin entered into the world and through sin death" with Wis 2:24: "By the envy of the devil, death entered the world."

15 "Known" in the pregnant biblical sense of spiritual experience.

16 In his commentary, Father Huby abandons Father Lagrange's explanation and adopts what is called the "historical interpretation." As a matter of fact, the interpretation I adopt is no less historical; one must, however, begin history, as does Scripture, with man's creation and not merely with his sin (see Huby, *op. cit.*, pp. 605–7). By this thesis, St. Paul apparently also wished to combat the Jewish concept that, according to the Palestinian Targum, attributes Adam's "justice" to the observation of the Law, identified there with the tree of life.

17 See *Summa Theol.* I–II, q. 89, a. 6, c. (Quotations from the *Summa* are taken from the translation of the Fathers of the English Dominican Province, New York: Benziger, 1947 [Translator].)

18 See Gn 3:13. Surely, St. Paul is alluding to this verse in 2 Cor 11:3 and 1 Tim 2:14, and in both cases he uses *exapatan*, the same composite verb used in Rom 7:11, rather than the simple *apatan* of the Septuagint.

19 "By the works of the law no human being shall be justified before him, for through law comes the recognition of sin" (Rom. 3:20).

20 Following entirely different lines of investigation, Father Gilleman reaches the same conclusion: "In the case of sin, the transgression of law formally specifies the sin, but its malice derives from its infidelity to charity. . . . This transgression is only the moral and exterior aspect of an actual disorder in our power of loving." Similarly, "moral obedience to law is rather the exterior aspect, the necessary mediation of our authentic and profound life which is love, so that moral life can be defined only by reference to charity." (Gerard Gilleman, S.J., *The Primacy of Charity in Moral Theology*, trans. William F. Ryan, S.J., and André Vachon, S.J. [Westminster: Newman, 1959], p. 279.)

21 This is particularly true of the commentary on Romans, which was the only one St. Thomas had time to finish. The rest, from 1 Cor 7:14 (or, more precisely, from 10:1) is a transcript of Brother Reginald, reflecting courses given between 1259 and 1265 at the papal court in Orvieto.

22 In Rom 7:14 St. Paul qualified the Old Law as *pneumatikos*.

82

²³ *In Hebr.*, cap. 8, lect. 2; *In 2 Cor.*, cap. 3, lect. 2.

²⁴ See Joseph Lécuyer, "Pentecôte et loi nouvelle," *La vie spirituelle*, 25 (May 1953), 471–90; also Jean Daniélou, S.J., *The Bible and the Liturgy* (Notre Dame: University of Notre Dame Press, 1956), pp. 330–32.

²⁵ *In Rom.* 8:2: *Haec lex Spiritus vitae est Dei Spiritus, quem humana mens legis vice accipit.* As is well known, far from being unreliable as a theologian, Seripando was created a cardinal in order that he might preside over the sessions of the Council of Trent as a legate, replacing Cardinal Cervini who had become Pope Marcellus II. See Hubert Jedin, *Papal Legate at the Council of Trent, Cardinal Seripando* (London: Herder, 1947), pp. 562–77.

²⁶ See Albert Descamps, *Les justes et la justice dan les évangiles et le christianisme primitif* (Louvain: Université catholique, 1950), pp. 112–13.

²⁷ *In 2 Cor.*, cap. 3, lect. 2. Likewise, St. Augustine's *Dilige et quod vis fac*, "Love and do what you will," seems to be, at first sight, a practical principle of conduct concerning fraternal love. (See J. Gallay, *Recherches de Science Religieuse* [1955], pp. 545–55.)

²⁸ In Rom 8:14 St. Paul gives this definition of a son of God: "Whoever are led by the Spirit of God, they are the sons of God."

²⁹ See Ferdinand Prat, S.J., *The Theology of St. Paul*, trans. John L. Stoddard (New York: Benziger, 1934), II, 312.

³⁰ On this particular aspect, see the excellent remarks of Gaston Salet in "La loi dans nos coeurs," *Nouvelle Revue Théologique*, 79 (1957), 449–62, 561–78.

³¹ What St. Paul means by this "law of Christ" ought to be sufficiently clear from what has just been said.

³² *Summa Theol.* I–II, q. 106, a. 1, c.

³³ See St. Augustine, *De Spiritu et Littera*, chaps. 14, 17, 19, *passim* (PL 44:215–22).

³⁴ *Summa Theol.* I–II, q. 106, a. 2, c. St. Thomas did not shrink from using the formula *sola fides,* so much abused later on. Commenting on 1 Tim 1:8: *Scimus quia bona est lex, si quis ea legitime utatur*, "We know that the Law is good, if a man uses it rightly," he explains that St. Paul has in mind the commandments of the Decalogue and intends to say that their legitimate use consists in not attributing to them what they do not contain. The Angelic Doctor writes: *Non est in eis spes justificationis, sed in sola fide*, "There is no hope of justification in them, but in faith alone," that is to say, *fides per caritatem operans*, "faith which works through charity" (Gal 5:6), of which he speaks so often. As a proof, he quotes precisely the famous verse of Rom 3:28: *Arbitramur enim justificari hominem per fidem sine operibus legis*, "We reckon that a man is justified by faith independently of the works of the Law" (see *In 1 Tim.*, lect. 3).

³⁵ In Rom 3:27 St. Paul opposes the law that consists of performing works to the one that consists in believing. (See St. Augustine, *op. cit.*, chap. 13, PL 44:213–15.)

³⁶ St. Robert Bellarmine, *De justificatione impii*, Liber I, caput XIX, *Opera Omnia* (Naples, 1856–62), IV, 492.

³⁷ To cite but one example, it is said that in the thirteenth century the pious King of France, St. Louis, attended several Masses every day and recited the Office, but he only received Communion three times a year.

³⁸ To use St. Thomas's expression (see *Summa Theol.* I–II, q. 108, a. 1, c.).

³⁹ The Greek verb *plēroun*, "fulfill," must be given here the meaning I mentioned earlier.

⁴⁰ As Father Huby puts it, the Christian, though freed from the Law, can by his own will call this freedom into question. "He can again live 'according to

the flesh' (Rom. 8:13), let sin reign in him (see 6:12); in doing so he is no longer under grace, but under the law. Then the law becomes again what it was for him before his union with Christ" (*op. cit.*, p. 233).

⁴¹ See Jean Mouroux, *The Christian Experience*, trans. George Lamb (New York: Sheed and Ward, 1954), pp. 138–39, 196–97.

⁴² With Kierkegaard, and against Scheler and Kant, Father Gillon rightly remarks that human love, too, experiences the need to bind itself. Only through a bond does love become stable and in part escapes contingency; for a Catholic, love escapes contingency altogether through the sacrament of marriage. The "institution," far from being hostile to love, saves it. (See *Angelicum* [1957], p. 257, n. 2.)

⁴³ See *Summa Theol.* I–II, q. 108, a. 1. See also a. 2: *Rectus usus gratiae est per opera caritatis,* "The right use of grace is through the works of love."

⁴⁴ The Gospel furnishes a typical example of outwitting the Law with regard to the Corban, "Something set apart for God" (see Mk 7:9–13). It has been said that, at times, the knowledge of the Law became "the knowledge of the means a just man may take in order to achieve his objectives without committing any fault against the Law." (Jacques Dupont, *Gnosis. La connaissance religieuse dans les épîtres de Saint Paul* [Louvain: Université catholique, 1949], p. 256.) Some Christians entertain an attitude toward the law of abstinence, for example, that is not far removed from the one Father Dupont describes.

⁴⁵ See Gilleman, *op. cit.*, p. 279: "The Christian way of considering law as the exteriority of love and of the moral order shows that the substance of moral life is not obedience to law, but charity towards persons, the human superior, and God; obedience, however indispensable, is second to love. . . . This 'law of grace' (Rom 6:15) is no longer a heavy yoke imposed from the outside; it is required by charity as its necessary determination."

⁴⁶ See Salet, *loc. cit.*, p. 575; Gillon, *loc. cit.*, pp. 376–77.

⁴⁷ 1QS vi 6–7. See Géza Vermès, *Discovery in the Judean Desert* (New York: Desclée, 1956), p. 143.

⁴⁸ Charles de Foucauld, *Ecrits Spirituels*, p. 171. Cf. the practical commentary given by Father René Voillaume in "Message from Beni-Abbès" of February 23, 1950, in *Seeds of the Desert*, trans. Willard Hill (Chicago: Fides, 1955), pp. 102–3.

⁴⁹ As we know, for St. Thomas sin is an offense against God only in so far as it is opposed to man's true welfare: *Non enim Deus a nobis offenditur nisi ex eo quod contra nostrum proprium bonum agimus.* (*Summa Contra Gentiles*, III, c. 122.)

⁵⁰ *In 2 Cor.*, cap. 3, lect. 3. ("His inner dynamism makes him do" is Father Lyonnet's interesting rendering of St. Thomas's: *Ex bono habitu inclinatur* [Translator].) See also *Summa Theol.* I–II, q. 108, a. 1, ad 2: "Since the grace of the Holy Ghost is like an interior habit bestowed on us and inclining us to act aright, it makes us do freely those things that are becoming to grace, and shun what is opposed to it."

⁵¹ See *Summa Contra Gentiles*, IV, c. 22.

⁵² Franciscus de Sylvestris Ferrariensis, *Comment. in Libros Quattuor contra Gentiles S. Thomae de Aquino*, lib. IV, cap. 22, 4.

VII. FREEDOM

The Word of God

For the Law, having but a shadow of the good things to come, and not the exact image of objects, is never able by the sacrifices which they offer continually, year after year the same, to perfect those who draw near; for in that case would they not have ceased to be offered, because the worshippers, once cleansed, would no longer have any consciousness of sin? Yet in these sacrifices sins are brought to remembrance year by year. For it is impossible that sins should be taken away with blood of bulls and of goats. Therefore in coming into the world, he says, "Sacrifice and oblation thou wouldst not, but a body thou hast fitted to me: In holocausts and sin-offerings thou hast had no pleasure. Then said I, 'Behold, I come—(in the head of the book it is written of me)—to do thy will, O God.'" In saying in the first place, "Sacrifices and oblations and holocausts and sin-offerings thou wouldst not, neither hast thou had pleasure in them" (which are offered according to the Law), and then saying, "Behold I come to do thy will, O God," he annuls the first covenant in order to establish the second. It is in this "will" that we have been sanctified through the offering of the body of Jesus Christ once for all.

And every priest indeed stands daily ministering, and often offering the same sacrifices, which can never take away sins; but Jesus, having offered one sacrifice for sins, has taken his seat forever at the right hand of God, waiting thenceforth until his enemies be made the footstool under his feet. For by one offering he has perfected forever those who are sanctified. Thus also the Holy Spirit testifies unto us. For after having said, "This is the covenant that I will make with them after those days, says the Lord: I will put

my laws upon their hearts, and upon their minds I will write them,"
he then adds, "And their sins and their iniquities I will remember
no more." Now where there is forgiveness of these, there is no
longer offering for sin.

Since then, brethren, we are free to enter the Holies in virtue
of the blood of Christ, a new and living way which he inaugurated
for us through the veil (that is, his flesh), and since we have a high
priest over the house of God, let us draw near with a true heart in
fullness of faith, having our hearts cleansed from an evil conscience
by sprinkling, and the body washed with clean water. Let us hold
fast the confession of our hope without wavering, for he who has
given the promise is faithful. And let us consider how to arouse one
another to charity and good works; not forsaking our assembly as
is the custom of some, but exhorting one another, and this all the
more as you see the Day drawing near.

(Hebrews 10:1–25)

GABRIEL MORAN, F.S.C.

Freedom in Christian Revelation

The genial reader will find in this comprehensive essay a discussion
of questions such as these: Is Christianity a religion of freedom?
How is human freedom related to the doctrine of creation? Why is
the God of freedom the Lord of history? Why did primitive man
fear time and history? How does faith free man from the uncertainties of history? Does God respect human freedom in his dialogue with man? Are the Old Testament and the Greek ideas of
freedom the same? Can Christ be called the man of faith? Does
proximity to God destroy freedom? Was Christ free in relation to
the past? The present? The future? Why did Christ's use of free-

Reprinted with permission from *The Proceedings of the Society of Catholic
College Teachers of Sacred Doctrine,* 1965.

dom create tension in the society about him? Why is violence vul-
nerable in the face of inner freedom? How does Christ's death set
men free? Why is the Christian free from the law? Does Christian
freedom admit of laws for the common good? Is freedom risky?
Should the Christian always obey without question? How does truth
make us free? How can the Christian create freedom for others?

Brother Gabriel Moran teaches in the graduate department of
catechetical theology at Manhattan College, New York. He is the
author of *Scripture and Tradition* and *Theology of Revelation.*

In his excellent little work of some years ago, *The Drama of
Atheist Humanism,* Henri de Lubac raised the question of how
it was possible that the religion first preached as joy, salvation, and
freedom should be felt to be an insupportable burden by modern
man. For it is a fact that since the nineteenth century Christianity
has been attacked not in the name of reason but in the name of and
in defense of freedom.

Of course, the Christian protests that this is all wrong. He claims
that Christianity has been misunderstood; that Christianity, far
from being the enemy of freedom, can alone provide a solid basis
for the establishment and preservation of man's freedom. The Christian claims, in other words, that modern secularism has ingested
into itself a corrupted form of Christian revelation against which it
must struggle. That may well be true; but this very fact makes the
Christian's task all the more difficult. It is not that the men of this
world have never heard of the freedom in Christian revelation;
rather, they have heard it and heard it again from the lips of
Christians, and they are sick to death of hearing words. For the
freedom which is spoken of by Christians seems esoteric and remote
from the demand for freedom which rings out throughout our world
today. The "freedom of the sons of God" so confidently spoken of
by exegetes of the Pauline epistles seems to men of this era at best
irrelevant and at worst a cruel play on words.

Part of our difficulty, I believe, is that discussion on the Christian
notion of freedom very often starts with St. Paul and ends with St.
Paul. It is true that only Paul among all the biblical writers developed an explicit doctrine of freedom. Nevertheless, to appreciate
his teaching it must be placed within a wider context and an historical development. The freedom concept in Galatians and Romans
is the capping stone of an understanding of freedom which begins

in the earliest books of the Old Testament and slowly evolves toward a formulation in the Trinitarian and Christological doctrine that formed the foundation of Western man's realization of the dignity and freedom of man.

I would like to begin, therefore, by examining the implicit foundations of freedom as they emerge in the Old Testament and carry through into the New. The explicit statement of this doctrine is, as I have said, in the Epistles of St. Paul. But between these two, Old Testament and St. Paul, is the key which connects them, the revelation of freedom itself in the person of Jesus Christ. Strangely enough, for all its talk about freedom, Catholic writing has for the most part left unexamined the freedom of him who embodies all that was best in the Old Testament tradition and who at the same time was the archetype and model for St. Paul's teaching on the freedom of a son of God. I will conclude with a few practical considerations for us based on St. Paul's teaching.

Turning first to the Old Testament, I will speak of the condition for the possibility of freedom and then the actuality and the historical development of freedom. The Old Testament has almost nothing to say about freedom, yet it is the history of the rise of freedom, for it was the introduction into humanity of a unique and novel conception of God and man. Freedom could never have been established by the teaching of the schools, by the writing of constitutions, by guarantees of economic security. All these must eventually have their place if freedom is to survive, but the first prerequisite of freedom was a true understanding of God and man's relation to God.

Without hesitation, wavering, or doubt, the testimony that underpins the whole Judaic-Christian revelation is that man finds his true self in relationship and only in relationship. Man has always been tempted and always will be tempted to seek his personal autonomy by separation, by removing from his surroundings whatever limits him, and by building a wall of security to protect the little he can call his own.

The reason that the Bible speaks confidently of man's discovery of himself in the giving up of himself resides in its peculiar understanding of God. Religions and their gods have not always stood on the side of man's freedom and personalization. They have more often than not fulfilled Marx's definition of religion as the "cry of the oppressed creature, the moan of a heartless world, the spirit of spiritless conditions, the opium of the people." But Judaic-Christian revelation, instead of being the perfection of religion as Marx claimed, would be more accurately described as the opposite of religion. The one unending strain that unifies the Bible is the announcement that man is no longer to search for the gods, that religion is at an end. Man cannot find God because God has first found him. The one, the absolute, Yahweh has spoken: "This day I have chosen you. I will be your God and you shall be my people."

The God who speaks to the Jewish people combines in his person the almost uncombinable properties of absolute transcendence over history and intimate involvement in the struggles of man's history. Infinite freedom had freely chosen to make man his *thou*. As the brilliant work of Erich Przywara [1] has shown, this delicate balance and irresolvable tension of God's immanence and transcendence is what specifies Christianity. Any deviation or imbalance, any misplaced emphasis on either side can only degrade the Christian understanding of God and man. Unfortunately, this balance and interrelationship cannot be maintained simply by asserting it, but must be dialectically worked out and always in process of being worked out historically, philosophically, theologically, and pastorally.

On the one hand, Yahweh is the supreme and absolute ruler who has no need of man. He can graciously bestow his presence precisely because he is self-sufficient. His transcendence is not one of reason over history or unchanging spirit over against matter; it is instead a transcendence of absolute authority. All depends upon him; nothing can frustrate his will.

Although the doctrine of creation emerges relatively late in the Old Testament, it could not help but come eventually. From the start Yahweh is without comparison; next to him all other gods are as nothing. The direction of Israelite thought was inevitable. "Our God is the one God; the Lord of this history is the Lord of all history. The one who spoke to us and saved us is the ruler and creator of mankind."

With the doctrine of creation there was established the metaphysical presupposition of human freedom. For "true freedom," writes Eric Frank,

> is conceivable only on the basis of the idea of creation. For this concept implies that the absolute cause, God, has posited vis-à-vis himself free beings who, in their very freedom, realize their true and necessary

existence, their destiny on this world. Only if man believes in the possibility of such inner freedom which is stronger than all worldly necessity, can he be certain that whenever he obeys with utter sincerity the voice of his conscience he will follow out the intention of creation.[2]

An ultimate relation to anything other than an absolute and infinite person, that is, a creator God, would destroy the possibility of freedom and would exhaust man in the search for finite goods.

The possibility of freedom, however, is not the same as freedom and the assertion of an absolute beyond the universe is not the achievement of an existing human freedom. For freedom to be actually attained it was not sufficient that God reign above the heavens; it was also necessary that he take active part in human history. The question of freedom is inextricably the question of man's history. Thus we have the other pole of the dialectic: the God of freedom is the Lord of history.

There is in modern theological writing, whether Catholic or Protestant, no more common an assertion than that of the historical nature of Judaic-Christian revelation. Anyone familiar with catechetical and liturgical literature knows that it is now almost axiomatic that revelation is to be presented as a "salvation history." Few people would deny that this is an improvement over past presentations of revelation. Some might have the uneasy feeling, however, that history is just another category into which revelation has been placed while there is yet no deep penetration into the nature of revelation itself. There is history to revelation not because God chose a good pedagogical instrument but simply because one of the partners in the revelatory relationship was man. God chose man for his beloved, and to choose man was to choose history.

Because history is not something outside man, because man *is* his history, then God's entrance into history means that God took hold of man in the real experience which men have of their own temporality. There is a sense in which all religions claim a revelation and even a revelation in time, but the time in non-Jewish religions is a mythical time, a transcendent instant at the beginning.[3] For the Israelites, on the contrary, the temporal, bodily, social situation acquired real meaning and religious value. God, who dominates and transcends all space and time, had freely chosen to enter the spatiotemporal situation of the community of man.

This understanding of God and time implies an entire anthropology. Man in his temporal and bodily mode of existence is the one that is related to God. It is not a mind or a soul or an atemporal spark of the divine that must answer to God; it is man, the temporal being, who must answer. There had always been time to man's existence but because time means change and change means decay and death, time was too frightening for man to face. Amazing as it might seem, man has for the most part tried to deny the existence of time and thereby of history, man's self-understanding in time. Mircea Eliade, in particular, has shown that primitive man fled from the terror of history and defended himself against all novelty by means of ritual and law.[4] But to escape from his own history was to flee from his own life; to refuse history was to refuse his own freedom. The replacement of freedom by tradition, law, and magical rite was a necessity; for mankind of itself has never been capable of bearing the burden of freedom. It was only through faith in the one who gives meaning to time that man was given the ability to face and accept his real, temporal life and thereby to discover that he was free.

All of this the Old Testament summarizes under the image of *word.* God addressed man personally and the reception by man of God's gift was the unveiling of their intersubjective relationship. A word is that which is addressed to a person as an invitation to communion through the awakening within him of the realization of his dignity and freedom. God's speech was the acts of fidelity and love that gave man the courage to trust in another and break the bonds of his own making that separated him from freedom. God's actions enabled man to recognize himself as lovable and to face his own condition so as to seek a meaning for the flux and apparent decadence of time.

Every act of love on God's part, every response on man's part, changed the revelatory relationship. As man came to accept his own self by entrusting himself to the partner in dialogue, the reality of God became clearer to him and at the same time his own destiny became clearer. Every recognized and accepted act of love threw light upon man's past and opened possibilities for man's future. Saved from the torturing anxieties of past faults and future uncertainties, man could become more truly present to God, to his neighbor and to himself.

What is true, unfortunately, of all personal relationships is preeminently true in the revelatory relation of God and man, namely, it is possible that despite a successful beginning one partner may turn back upon himself and refuse to give himself to the other. From the first moment of their dialogue God knew the weakness of man. He knew that despite all the divine testimonies of love and fidelity man would draw back and prefer a way that looked easier. An education of man to freedom could not help but be a slow, halting, and somewhat painful process in which God and man became "accustomed" to one another.

Every time that man said "no," God's "yes" remained steadfast; not that God's affirmation overran man's freedom but that God kept finding a new starting point from which to move and a new route to follow in the dialogue with man. God had bound himself to the limitations of his partner; he had made himself weak to save the weak. The most amazing thing about the revelatory process is that the sins of men did not break off the process but were in one sense part of the process. Man's rebellion simply became the occasion of new revelatory action on God's part. Unlike a human partner whose love and patience are finite, God refused to leave man to the selfishness that would destroy his freedom. God knew that he must gently draw man forward, not simply by disregarding failure, but by using even failure to reveal the relation between man and God and the road to true freedom.[5]

To summarize this Old Testament revelation of freedom, we may contrast it to the Greek concept of a free man. In ancient classical thought—and in modern rationalist counterparts—freedom is attained by submission to universal laws of reason. The temporal, bodily, social activities of history are outside of freedom. Without depth of meaning history inevitably becomes cyclical repetition. Man's *reason* becomes free, that is, the reason of the élite who can free their minds from bodily needs and desires and can attain to the knowledge of the laws of the universe. There is a naive sense of the power of man to control his own destiny limited only by the limitations of his knowledge.[6]

The Jews in regard to freedom speak less but do more. Their concern is not man's reason but man; their end is not an ideal human nature but a living human community. Their intention was not to free man from his body but to free man from himself, not to create an intellectual élite but to summon every man to responsibility. What the Old Testament demands is that man give up his petty, defensive tactics to protect his diminishing freedom, that he submit with an absolute submission to the only One who can set him free. Old Testament revelation is the call to every man to join in the communal march of humanity toward freedom.

All other religion had failed. Either the gods were finite and struggling like man and the worship paid to such gods was, in Nietzsche's words, the flowing out of man into the robber behind the clouds; or else the gods were pure and exalted but man was left without faith or hope and thus could not escape from the entanglements of the past and the meaninglessness of the future. What was needed by all but what was found only by Israel was hope, that is, the confident movement toward a final point at which a community of free men would be established.

In Israel itself, however, men refused to go forward to the communion which would free them. They defended themselves against God with a variety of means, even the written word of God. To the most clear-sighted among them it was still not certain how the process would end, whether the last word would be one of wrath or love.[7] But, finally, out of the few who represented the best of Israelite tradition there emerged from the community, flesh of our flesh, the one who could bear the final gift of God's personal existence. The end had been reached and the end was Christ.

That Jesus Christ not only brought the revelation of God but that he *is* the revelation of God is often said today. To say this, however, does not guarantee a truly Christocentric understanding of revelation. That God was in Christ revealing himself to man and that Jesus Christ is God's word to the world is an affirmation repeatedly made in Catholic writing. That the man Jesus was the recipient of God's revelation and that he fulfilled the vocation of the man of faith is a statement which is equally important yet seldom made in Catholic theological writing. Even while asserting that Christ is the revelation, Catholic treatises still place the reception of revelation in the apostolic experience. But if Christ is truly the union of God and man, if he possesses a true human consciousness, then he is the participating subject who receives God's self-disclosure for his brothers in his consciousness and freedom.

To say then that Christ lived by vision but that his followers live by faith is true but may be misleading. If one conceives of faith as the patient acceptance of what God wills over what man desires, Jesus' fundamental attitude is the same as that of the true servant of Yahweh and the faithful Christian. When we imitate him and follow him on the road of obedience we enter faith most deeply. Though he did not possess the theological virtue of faith, he is nevertheless the archetype and ideal of faith. His knowledge was measured by his mission; he lived in the sheer, naked, unqualified acceptance of what came from the Father.[8]

Christ's vision was not a point of command but a point of receptivity wherein he possessed eternal life as a gift from the Father. He completed the lineage of promise, faith, and prophecy; and in his face was revealed the truly religious man. To a world seeking freedom by the establishment of self-autonomy Jesus remains the unsurpassable testimony that not only is freedom not destroyed by proximity to God but that man is constituted in freedom precisely insofar as he is present to God. Jesus is the living proof that man is freedom for God.

From the beginning of the universe God had been preparing the world for this gift which was beyond hope and yet awaited. By successive acts of freeing Israel from her selfish ways, God had prepared within mankind a center of consciousness for the reception of a definitive act of love that would set men free. By Jesus' complete receptivity to the self-bestowing love of God all that had been haltingly and successively made present in the history of Israel was contracted into a single life-span. He lived a real human history with the understanding of his past and the projection of his future. Because he was free he could face the past with openness, finding in the Old Testament the elements for his own mission. Because of his complete submission to the Father, he was free to criticize the traditions of the past. He was able to distinguish the permanent development of man's freedom before God from, on the one side, lawlessness and, on the other side, human precepts which had become rigid and stultifying.

Toward the future his attitude was also unencumbered by fear or narrowness. Because of his complete trust in the Father he could live without anxiety though he had not where to lay his head. He did not settle down in his parish synagogue but moved over the countryside, blurring those distinctions of place and place, class and class, which men build for their private security; he was even accused of making everyone his neighbor and respectable people just do not do such things. He called for followers who would put their trust in God rather than in man, who would resolutely look to the future with hope.

Thus freed from the anxieties of past and future, thus perceiving the veiled meaning of past and future in God's revelatory love of the present, Jesus was the man who lived in the present. Present to himself, present to other men, present to God; such is the meaning of freedom and love. Freed from all egocentric concern and completely open to what the present moment offered, Jesus was the man for others, the man for all men.[9] He was present to them in service, drawing forth their freedom. Although his position liberated him from some of the bonds of nature he did not use his miraculous powers for overcoming others but only for service. He did not claim status for himself but wished only to be accepted as the one sent from the Father, as the promised son of Israel, son of man.

The question of freedom is always the question of history, that is, of a human history in progressive liberation from itself. Christ was *perfect* man, yet he was truly *man*, journeying from the bondage of flesh to the freedom of spirit. He gained his knowledge and freedom in the slow and often painful return to the Father. Though he was son of God he learned obedience by the things he suffered. He grew in wisdom and freedom before God and man and though desirous of spreading his freedom to all men, he had during his lifetime to be content with working outward from a motley group of disciples. Day by day he grew clearer in his consciousness of what his mission would demand. Daily he made the choices which issued from his freedom and committed that freedom to a course from which there was no turning back.

His freedom created a tension in the society about him. To be a free man in a fearful, sinful race of men is a terrifying thing. Sin was forced out into the open by this man. Demons always seemed to show up when he was in the vicinity. He repeatedly claimed that he had come to set men free but he seemed to disregard the fact that men could not endure freedom. They could bear neither the dizzying and frightening spectacle of their own lives unprotected by rituals, nor the presence of another whose freedom was a continuing reproach to their own selfishness.

The gospel ending is perhaps less surprising to our generation because we have seen what happens when men who are free of pettiness and egocentricity stand defenselessly and nonviolently for the rights and freedom which belong to their brothers. When such freedom appears there is drawn forth into the open all the fear and violence that has festered beneath the surface encysted in the heart of man. Sinful man is frightened by freedom, he is frightened by love, and most of all he is frightened by God. The one time in our history, therefore, that the divine in all its freedom and love appeared on our earth there could be little doubt of what the result would be: men killed him.

The story of Christ's life, therefore, moves inexorably to its climax. All of the acts of partial freedom which constituted his history were preparations for the final gift of self that would set him entirely free. As his life recapitulated the history of his people so the final act of his life recapitulated his own history. If his death was the supreme revelatory event of God's plan it was also the supreme act of participating receptivity on the part of man. With cries of bitter agony in the garden and on the cross he passed through the dark night of the soul to the final reception of revelation and freedom. He had entered the struggle on behalf of the destiny of mankind; having perceived the truth of this destiny and having recognized what was demanded to set man free, he followed the will of his Father obedient unto the death of the cross. He ascended the cross as man's answer to God but not without suffering, fear, and the desire to let the chalice pass. "We are astounded," writes Durrwell, "we are shocked by this weakness and longing; it would have been more heroic, we feel, to accept unmoved this death which was to save the world. But this astonishment is born of a lack of understanding. We forget that the drama of mankind in search of salvation was first played out in Christ." [10]

So it was with the charismatics before him, so also it has been with men who have stood for freedom after him; the force of evil always seems to be more powerful. To fight violence with nonviolence has always seemed a rather absurd business. But the force of evil and violence, for all its blustering show, has a devastating vulnerability. It does not stand in the truth and therefore it is not free. It has no flexibility, no capacity for give and take. It must fight with blind instinct, knowing that if the least entrance is given to love and freedom there is no telling what might happen. It cannot see that within itself lies the seed of self-contradiction and self-destruction, for the more it tries to stamp out freedom, the more it wounds itself and draws forth further heroism from those it hopes to conquer. And finally, at the very moment when evil seems surely

to have triumphed, when the man who sought for love and freedom lies shot in his automobile, beaten on the street, or hanged upon
a cross, it is precisely then that the full power of freedom is cut
loose. For one thing is sure about the power of freedom: if it does
not conquer in life then it will most certainly conquer in death. And
for the supreme liberation of man that God desired, only death
was sufficiently powerful. Christ could have gotten a wonderful
response and a complete submission by coming down from the cross
to meet the taunts of his challengers; but he would only have succeeded in making cowardly men cower still more. Instead Christ
chose the long, painful, worthless-looking way of love and obedience
because he knew that this was the way to set men free.

His death, therefore, was the passageway to spirit and freedom;
what was death from our side was from the Father's side resurrection. Opening himself completely to all truth, Christ was transformed by the inrushing Spirit. Bowing his head, writes St. John, he
passed on the Spirit. He became free for all men, not the men of
Palestine in the year 30, but free for all men of all time. Having
conquered sin and death, he could manifest in his human nature
that liberty and joy, that availability and transparency, which make
him present when we call upon him in Eucharistic assembly.[11]
Entering into his glory he became the revelatory-redemptive principle of God's activities with man. He passed beyond time to become
the center of time; he reached the end of time by contracting time
within his person. He is the unfailing promise and first installment
of the revelatory freedom that is meant for all mankind.

St. Paul's doctrine of the freedom of the sons of God emerges
from reflection upon this Old Testament history and its culmination
in Jesus Christ. It was a dangerous doctrine that Christ had
preached, and not only preached but lived, namely, that people
come first and that abstract rules are measured by people and not
vice versa. And it was Paul who saw most clearly that there was no
turning back on this road. Once the person of Jesus Christ had revealed what the person is meant to be, once the road to freedom
had been opened up by the Spirit, Paul recognized that man was
now faced with a more serious and radical option: either to live
with all the risks of freedom or else to violate human dignity.

There were other men, of course, who whispered to Paul: "Let's
take it easy. People are not quite ready for freedom. At least let us

keep some protective barriers from the Old Law and we will phase these out in due and deliberate time." One thing which Paul saw clearly and unerringly and which many of his contemporaries and many of his descendants have not seen, is that the time process is irreversible. The passage of Jesus Christ and the outpouring of his Spirit was something genuinely novel in the history of our race. With Christ the law as a collection of rules to be followed was destroyed. He did not qualify the law by love; he abolished it. What was excusable before Christ, what could even be a pedagogical instrument leading up to Christ, could only be blasphemy after him. Once he had given us the model on which to base our morality, once he had given us the power that enables us to be moral and free, then to hope that law is the means to salvation is to deny that Christ has saved us. All those old laws, every law made by man or God, has been swallowed up by Christ.

If you still wish to speak of law, says St. Paul, I am willing to say that there is one law: the law is Christ. But remember that the relation of man to this law is almost the exact reverse of his relation to other law. This law does not stand over against man demanding things which man thinks he should be able to do but just never seems to succeed in doing. This law is the inner power, accomplishing with us and in us what we never dreamed ourselves capable of doing. But we cannot have it both ways; we cannot give the Spirit a chance to operate while we cling to the security of the old laws. Nor can we take the beautiful teachings and ideals of Christ and simply use them to modify our old human safeguards. The law of the gospel, said St. Thomas, will kill you if it is not infused by the Spirit.[12]

We like to think that our gifts, our works, our talents are the highest things we can offer to God and our fellow man; but that is what is wrong: they are things. We cannot seem to understand that God does not want this or that work while we remain the same; he wants us so that he can kill us in the flesh and bring us to life in the Spirit. All our patch sewing and dike repairing is useless, says Paul; what we must first do is relax, let go and trust. Unfortunately, we who know that mankind has been set free from fear are in many ways frightened people and our fears have hardened into our attitudes and our corporate structure.[13] Thus we tend to read St. Paul with the presupposition that he could not have seriously meant what he seems to say. At any rate, St. Paul did not know the rules of religious orders, the touchy feelings of certain rich benefactors, and a thousand practical considerations that we have to keep in mind. Surely Paul would be a more practical and reasonable man if he were alive today—or would he?

As a matter of fact St. Paul did not have such an easy time in his own day with this doctrine of freedom. He was accused of all things of being immoral, of preaching laxity and license. This is not so surprising, however; if anyone wishes never to be accused of immorality he should not preach the gospel. This is because those who do not accept the gospel of freedom find little room for neutrality and therefore must attack it. The remarkable thing is that the doctrine of freedom of the Spirit is attacked for advocating what it alone succeeds in avoiding. Men say they cannot base morality on the dignity of the person and Christian charity because that would make morality individualistic and subjectivistic. They have not understood at all what St. Paul was talking about. He did not ask for an individual self-sufficiency, arbitrary and whimsical in its choices. He wanted first of all an admission of insufficiency, a realization that the individual must give up all arbitrary and selfish aims. The Christian who lives with the freedom of the Spirit is one who lives *responsibly*, that is, receptive to the Spirit's working in the community. He knows that freedom is a gift and that he shares in the freedom meant for all the children of God. He knows that as soon as he begins to seek himself rather than God and the community he has lost this freedom.

In the actual, concrete working out of man's social existence, the community or representatives of the community must draw up rules, prescriptions, or if you like, laws. These prescriptions, whether civil or religious, are binding simply because the community needs them. The Christian who is living with the freedom of a son will fulfill these without their forcing him. Insofar as he is listening to the Spirit he is already doing much more. The question is not whether there are few or many prescriptions, whether they are positively or negatively phrased; the real issue is whether they are measured by the dignity of the human person in community and are constantly re-examined in their capacity to buttress personal existence. For the Christian this means ultimately whether all things are measured in the light of Jesus Christ and the human person as transformed by him. If someone now says that all this freedom talk does not make much difference because in the end we all have to follow the traffic regulations, and pay our income tax and keep away from the other man's wife, then he just has not understood at all what freedom means. And if that is so, perhaps it is because we who are explaining it have not yet understood it ourselves.

My summation of all this is that the Christian life is the life of freedom. It need be nothing more than that and it can certainly be nothing less. Freedom can be a burden, a terrible burden if men are not given the help and the education to live their freedom; but they must be helped to carry it, not stripped of their possession. Freedom is a risky business because the possibility of success here entails the possibility of failure; but man's freedom was God's choice, not ours. Given the human capacity to misunderstand and given human deceitfulness, which can misuse the best of things, the preaching of Christian freedom might entail some unfortunate side results. But instead of pulling back at this point, instead of authority panicking at the first abuse of freedom, the Christian ought to insist all the more strongly on the nature and necessity of Christian freedom. More importantly, he must embody in his own life the living proof that freedom *from* the constraint of all law is freedom *for* God and the community of mankind. Not all people would live up to this calling but at least we would be aiming at the right thing. If we were thoroughly committed to letting Catholic children grow up through responsiveness to God and man, if we did not base our moral teaching on threat and fear, if we did not replace their consciences with answers to cases, then there might well be—as some people fear—a good deal of hedonism and lawbreaking among them; but it would be possible for them to become thoroughly Christian. The question is whether the Christian teacher believes in the power of faith and love to attract men to the truth.

The unending testimony of the Bible from the Old Testament through the Apocalypse is that man will find his true self only by the radical submission of his whole temporal, bodily, and social existence to God. Man can attain to the possession of freedom only by handing it over totally to God and to no one else. It is as terribly simple as that and as terribly difficult. Of those persons who demand the submission of my freedom there are only three whom I can obey absolutely and without question: they are the Father, the Son, and the Holy Spirit. It so happens, however, that I never meet any one of these Three except through the mediation of the human. Both the divine demand and the distinction of divine from the instrument of mediation must be discerned by my intelligence. Neither the voice of my superior, nor the Church's teaching, nor the words of Holy Scripture, can be obeyed without question. I must always question, I must seek the meaning of every command and search out how this applies to my life. Or, rather, it is not merely a question of applying things in mechanical fashion but of discerning and even creating the truth in a situation where God is now revealing himself.

God is still speaking the Word in the human consciousness of Christ and the Spirit is still testifying in the heart of the Church. In a world of ambiguous grays where it is almost never a question of simple right and wrong but a question of the decisive thing demanded at this point in our lives, we must really be attentive to the revelatory action of God. Any human being who demands submission and obedience of me must be willing to listen, not so much to me but to the community, to Jesus Christ, and to his Holy Spirit. There is no need to make the exercise of authority impractical or unnecessarily complicated; the issue at stake is the fundamental attitudes of authority toward power, of the individual toward community, and of all toward God.

Accompanying the proper attitudes, there must be a continual search to discover how we are to serve God with our fellow man. Our society does differ from that of the first century in being more complex. It is a world in which individual actions can have far-reaching effects, a world in which the social structure can no longer be regarded as morally neutral.[14] It would be simplistic to suppose that we should get rid of all but the gospel and preach only a general law of love. Those who oppose moral legalism sometimes advocate this as an answer, but paradoxically, this can only lead to a new legalism and formalism.

St. Paul, while asserting that there is only one law, that of the charity of Christ, could become exceedingly practical and concrete in his moral teachings. For us to be equally practical it will require more effort and it will demand a study not only of Scripture and theology but of the contemporary sciences. We may regret that this should be so but Christ only said that the truth will set us free; he did not promise that the truth could be had without some effort.

Christ came to make men free; he was quite insistent on the point; the whole of Christian revelation is unmistakably clear. Yet at the end of all the theoretical analysis we are likely to feel even more dismayed than before. Our everyday life seems to bear so little resemblance to this doctrine of Christian freedom. This freedom is all so very nice but one person finds the superior has not heard about it and is not the least bit interested in listening; another would like to speak the truth but what if it means losing his job when he has little ones at home to feed; another has great desires to accomplish things for the kingdom of God but he is bound by psychological or physical handicaps that make everything he does seem worthless. Freedom always has its limitations in this world. There are no answers and no final resolutions to the conflicts which engage the Christian and it would be cruel to pretend that there are. Nevertheless, it seems to me that the one who has understood Paul's words can attain a basic freedom and peace amidst the most trying situations. "The life of a Christian ought to be like the ocean, with the surface constantly battered by storms, but miles and miles below deep peace, unmoved tranquility." [15]

If those in authority do not want to listen, if those with whom one is living are apathetic, then this is where freedom is most needed and where the testimony of the Spirit is to be made effective. The test of the true charismatic in the Church, writes Rahner,[16] comes when he finds no response or is rebuked. Then it is that he either builds a clique around himself in the community or else he continues to try to shed light and love upon the situation so as to create freedom for all. There is no freedom without truth and there is no truth without communication; and every one of us has the responsibility to speak to someone and to listen to everyone.

The Christian who is free will live the truth as he sees it while working with whatever intelligence and love he finds among superiors and equals; he will nurture that freedom and appeal to it. If he is forced, as the apostles were, to oppose a human authority he must do so with genuine respect and love for authority. At every step he must really listen, no matter how certain he is that he is right and the others are wrong.

God is speaking to his church. Freedom is alive and growing

and there is no force on earth that can stop it. The one weapon for which there is no match and which has never been surpassed is in the Christian's possession: the charity of Christ presses us.

References

[1] Erich Przywara, "St. Augustine and the Modern World," in *Monument to St. Augustine,* trans. E. I. Watkin (London: Sheed and Ward, 1945), pp. 251–86.

[2] Eric Frank, *Philosophical Understanding and Religious Truth* (New York: Oxford, 1945), p. 132.

[3] Henri-Charles Puech, "Gnosis and Time," in *Man and Time. Papers from the Eranos Yearbooks,* trans. Ralph Manheim (New York: Pantheon Books, 1957), p. 82.

[4] Mircea Eliade, *Cosmos and History,* trans. Willard Trask (New York: Harper Torchbook, 1959), p. 161.

[5] Romano Guardini, *Offenbarung* (Würzburg: Werkbund, 1940), p. 63.

[6] R. G. Collingwood, *The Idea of History* (Oxford: Clarendon Press, 1946), p. 24.

[7] Karl Rahner, *Theological Investigations,* trans. Cornelius Ernst (Baltimore: Helicon, 1961), I, 49.

[8] Hans Urs von Balthasar, *Martin Buber and Christianity,* trans. Alexander Dru (New York: Macmillan, 1962), p. 104.

[9] See: Erik Routley, *The Man for Others* (New York: Oxford, 1964).

[10] F. X. Durrwell, *The Resurrection,* trans. Rosemary Sheed (New York: Sheed and Ward, 1960), p. 57.

[11] Charles Moeller, "Is It Possible, in the Twentieth Century, To Be a Man of the Bible?" in *The Liturgy and the Word of God* (Collegeville, Minn.: Liturgical Press, 1959), p. 154.

[12] *Summa Theol.* I–II, q. 106, a. 2, c.; see Stanislas Lyonnet, "St. Paul: Liberty and Law," in *The Bridge,* IV (New York: Pantheon Books, 1962), p. 244.

[13] John Harmon, "Toward a Theology of the City Church," *Cross Currents,* 14 (Fall 1964), 407.

[14] Hans Urs von Balthasar, *Science, Religion and Christianity,* trans. Hilda Graef (Westminster: Newman, 1958), p. 76.

[15] Archbishop Michael Ramsey, as quoted in *God's Frozen People,* ed. Mark Gibbs and Ralph Morton (Philadelphia: Westminster, 1964), p. 187.

[16] Karl Rahner, *The Dynamic Element in the Church,* trans. W. J. O'Hara (New York: Herder and Herder, 1964), p. 78.

VIII. FORGIVENESS

The Word of God

And he said, "A certain man had two sons. And the younger of them said to his father, 'Father, give me the share of the property that falls to me.' And he divided his means between them.

"And not many days later, the younger son gathered up all his wealth, and took his journey into a far country; and there he squandered his fortune in loose living. And after he had spent all, there came a grievous famine over that country, and he began himself to suffer want. And he went and joined one of the citizens of that country, who sent him to his farm to feed swine. And he longed to fill himself with the pods that the swine were eating, but no one offered to give them to him.

"But when he came to himself, he said, 'How many hired men in my father's house have bread in abundance, while I am perishing here with hunger! I will get up and go to my father, and will say to him, Father, I have sinned against heaven and before thee. I am no longer worthy to be called thy son; make me as one of thy hired men.' And he arose and went to his father.

"But while he was yet a long way off, his father saw him and was moved with compassion, and ran and fell upon his neck and kissed him. And the son said to him, 'Father, I have sinned against heaven and before thee. I am no longer worthy to be called thy son.' But the father said to his servants, 'Fetch quickly the best robe and put it on him, and give him a ring for his finger and sandals for his feet; and bring out the fattened calf and kill it, and let us eat and make merry; because this my son was dead, and has come to life again; he was lost, and is found.' And they began to make merry."

"Now his elder son was in the field; and as he came and drew near to the house, he heard music and dancing. And calling one of the servants he inquired what this meant. And he said to him, 'Thy brother has come, and thy father has killed the fattened calf, because he has got him back safe.' But he was angered and would not go in.

"His father, therefore, came out and began to entreat him. But he answered and said to his father, 'Behold, these many years I have been serving thee, and have never transgressed one of thy commands; and yet thou hast never given me a kid that I might make merry with my friends. But when this thy son comes, who has devoured his means with harlots, thou hast killed for him the fattened calf.'

"But he said to him, 'Son, thou art always with me, and all that is mine is thine; but we were bound to make merry and rejoice, for this thy brother was dead, and has come to life; he was lost, and is found.' "

(Luke 15:11–32)

ANTHONY L. RUBSYS

The Parable of the Forgiving Father

The heartened reader will find in this brief but incisive commentary a discussion of questions such as these: How did the Old Testament speak of God's steadfast love? What are the three parables that Luke's Gospel gives of God's forgiveness? How does St. Paul stress God's mercy in his letter to Timothy? What special insight can be gained from Rembrandt's painting of the prodigal son? Why should the "parable of the prodigal son" be renamed? Why does this parable tell us about sin before it speaks of forgiveness? How is sin an alienation? A slavery? What does the parable tell us about human repentance? What does it tell us about God's attitude to the sinner? Why did Jesus accept table fellowship with sinners?

Father Anthony Rubsys, a graduate of the Pontifical Biblical Institute, teaches Sacred Scripture at Manhattan College in New York.

The contents of faith seem very disparate, but they possess a close unity. What is made known in the Book of the divine self-disclosure—the Bible—can be summed up in three words: God loves man. This love of God for man has been strikingly revealed in the context of human failure and divine forgiveness.

The love of God which breaks into the arena of the history of human failure in the Christ-event—promised and fulfilled—is a forgiving love. The Old Testament sums it up in song:

> Praise Yahweh, all you nations!
> Glorify him, all you peoples!
>
> For steadfast is his kindness (ḥesed) toward us,
> And the fidelity ('emeth) of Yahweh endures forever.
>   (Ps 117)

The Covenant Community of the Old Testament must have sung it with throbbing hearts in its teetering on the edge of the understanding of "salvation from" and "salvation for" and in its chasing the ever-receding horizon of the Promise in terms of the offspring, the land, and being "a blessing" to all the nations of the earth (cf. Gn 12:1–3).

The New Testament preserves for all times to come the happy memory and the self-expression of the New Israel—her faith and experience of the Father's forgiving love in Luke's drama of salvation: the lost sheep, the lost coin, and the prodigal son (cf. Lk 15:1–31)—"there is joy in heaven over one repentant sinner" (Lk 15:7, 10, 32). "Trustworthy and deserving of wholehearted acceptance is the saying, 'Christ Jesus came into the world to save sinners.' Of these I am at the head of the list" (1 Tim 1:15). "Thus to pray is good and acceptable in the sight of God our Savior, who wills that all men be saved and come to the knowledge of the truth" (1 Tim 2:3).

Parables are not history. They are simply stories whose whole purpose is to offer an insight into some truth. Frequently they are more important than any book of history ever written. And Jesus was the Master of teaching in parables. He taught important truths through interesting and easily remembered simple stories.[1]

Artists have a keener insight into the human and the divine than most men; they experience vicariously, as it were, the depths of the human-ness of man and the divine-ness of God. Rembrandt, for one, has discovered the true center of the parable of the prodigal son. His painting of the return of the prodigal son makes concrete God's forgiving concern for man in his fallenness. The serene tenderness of the reunion of the forgiving father and the prodigal son floods the painting. The father is central in it, the son is almost anonymous—his back is turned to the viewer! There emerges in the painting a certain emphasis, which forcefully directs the attention from the miserable state of the son to the joy of the forgiving father. Rembrandt has truly captured on canvas the true insight of this parable of Jesus—the father who forgives. No wonder—there is so much said in the parable about the joy of the father, and not a word about the joy of the son! It would be fitting, therefore, to rename the Lucan story as the parable of the forgiving father.[2]

As Jesus proclaims the forgiving Father by word and by action, and declares his goodness in his works, there arises in man an awareness of the distance of God and the fallenness of man, coupled with a desire for God. Man is provoked by Jesus' word and action to come to grips with the meaning of his existence in the light of the God who loves. And this is what is described in the parable of the forgiving father.

Man needs night in order to understand and appreciate day; he needs winter in order to understand and appreciate spring; illness in order to understand and appreciate health. To understand, to "stand-under," divine forgiveness one must understand human failure—sin.

The parable of the forgiving father shows what Jesus and his community of the New Testament understood by sin. "It is going out from the father's house, i.e., godlessness and remoteness from God working itself in a life in the world with all its desires and its filth "[3] Sin is not only man's failure against heaven and before God—"I have sinned against heaven and before you" (vv. 18, 21)—it is man's failure before himself; it is a defiant claim of independence, a going out from the father's house, a refusal to be the son of and an alienation from the loving father: "give me the part of the property that falls to my share . . . the younger son cashed everything and went off to a far-off country" (vv. 12, 13).

This going out from the Father's house—man's alienation—can be truly described as "a hurt to the Father," because it made the Father sad and deprived him of the presence of the son whom he loved.[4] Hence, joy upon the return of the son, "lost . . . and found again" (v. 23), "let us feast and celebrate" (v. 24)—the joy of the Father. Love yearns for nearness and communion. It is present in both the sadness of the departure and in the joy of the return.

The state of the son away from home is described as a slavery: "he went to throw himself at the mercy of a citizen of that region" (v. 15). His defiant claim of independence was only a feeling of freedom but not being free. There is a dramatic touch of irony. The citizen of that anonymous region "sent him to his farm to tend pigs" (v. 15). A Jewish fellow seems oddly out of place in "that region" where a pig farm is a legitimate pursuit of farmers.

The parable of the forgiving father also shows what Jesus and his community of the New Testament understood by forgiveness. In the light of the self-disclosure of God in and through Jesus, man is provoked to discover himself, his alienation from God, and his need to return to the Father. Jesus in the parable does not speak of sin and its nature and consequences, but is conscious of its reality. He proclaims God as the Father in his sovereignty, conscious that such a proclamation goes right home to the sin, and thus brings about the awareness of the need of a *metanoia* (i.e., repentance, literally "a change of mind").[5] Consequently, the forgiveness of sin includes necessarily the return of the alienated man to God in the sense of the *metanoia:* "there is joy in heaven over one repentant sinner" (v. 7; cf. vv. 10, 32).

The son does not face a reluctant father in order to obtain forgiveness. Quite the contrary, the father himself expects, hopes, provokes the return of the son.[6] The son was "still a good way off when his father caught sight of him and, stirred to pity, ran and threw his arms round his neck and kissed him affectionately" (v. 20) even before the son could make his confession!

The father of the parable never changes in his love for his son; God never changes in his love for man. The son of the parable is alienated, has alienated himself, and is in need of a return; the sinner is alienated, has alienated himself, from God and is in need of a return to God.

The sinner cannot return to God on his own, unless the Good Shepherd (cf. vv. 4–7) "goes in search of the one that was lost" (v. 4) and "puts [him] on his shoulders" (v. 5), and both together return to the Father. The Good Shepherd theme in the parables opens the redemptive dimensions of man's return to God. The attitude of the Good Shepherd is further described in the Synoptics: "it is my mission to call sinners, not saints" (Mt 9:13). He makes concrete the concern of the forgiving Father in word and in action; he is sent to those who live in the guilt of alienation far from God in order to call them to God. The result is expressed succinctly: "and it so happened that many tax collectors and sinners were reclining at table with Jesus and his disciples" (Mt 9:10; cf. also Mt 9:11–13; Lk 15:1, 2; 19:7). From this result stemmed the judgment about Jesus as "that boon companion of tax collectors and sinners" (Mt 11:19). The forgiveness of God thus has its "sacramental" dimensions, namely, the acceptance of Jesus of the table fellowship with sinners, "the closest fellowship known to the oriental world," [7] which is the effective sign of the reunion of the forgiving God and the fallen man. Man, in finding God through his forgiving love, finds himself, because the effect of such love "is to stimulate self-respect in the other person. Its concern is to help the one loved to become his true self. It seeks him for his own sake. In a mysterious way such love finds its purest realization in its power to stimulate the other to attain the highest self-realization. Thus its effect is to draw the other out into freedom." [8]

References

[1] Cf. Joachim Jeremias, *Die Gleichnisse Jesu* (München: Siebenstern Taschenbuch Verlag, 1965), pp. 9–14.

[2] Cf. Stanislas Lyonnet, *De Peccato et Redemptione* (Rome: Pontifical Biblical Institute, 1957), I, 61.

[3] Walter Grundmann, "Die Sünde im Neuen Testament," in Gerhard Kittel, ed., *Theologisches Wörterbuch zum Neuen Testament* (Stuttgart: Verlag von W. Kohlhammer, 1933), I, 306.

[4] Cf. Lyonnet, *op. cit.*, p. 62.

[5] Cf. Grundmann, *loc. cit.*

[6] Cf. Lyonnet, *loc. cit.*

[7] Grundmann, *loc. cit.*

[8] Romano Guardini, *The Faith and Modern Man* (New York: Pantheon Books, Inc., 1959), p. 31.

IX. PRUDENCE

The Word of God

And the Lord said, "Who, dost thou think, is the faithful and prudent steward whom the master will set over his household to give them their ration of grain in due time? Blessed is that servant whom his master, when he comes, shall find so doing. Truly I say to you, he will set him over all his goods. But if that servant says to himself, 'My master delays his coming,' and begins to beat the menservants and the maids, and to eat and drink, and to get drunk, the master of that servant will come on a day he does not expect, and in an hour he does not know, and will cut him asunder and make him share the lot of the unfaithful. But that servant who knew his master's will, and did not make ready for him and did not act according to his will, will be beaten with many stripes. Whereas he who did not know it, but did things deserving of stripes, will be beaten with few. But of everyone to whom much has been given, much will be required; and of him to whom they have entrusted much, they will demand the more.

"I have come to cast fire upon the earth, and what will I but that it be kindled? But I have a baptism to be baptized with; and how distressed I am until it is accomplished! Do you think that I came to give peace upon the earth? No, I tell you, but division. For henceforth in one house five will be divided, three against two, and two against three. They will be divided, father against son and son against his father; mother against daughter and daughter against the mother; mother-in-law against her daughter-in-law and daughter-in-law against her mother-in-law."

And he said also to the crowds, "When you see a cloud rising in the west, you say at once, 'A shower is coming,' and so it comes

*to pass. And when you see the south wind blow, you say, 'There
will be a scorching heat,' and so it comes to pass. You hypocrites!
you know how to judge the face of the sky and of the earth; but
how is it that you do not judge this time? But why even of your-
selves do you not judge what is right?"*

(Luke 12:42–57)

BERNARD HÄRING, C.SS.R.

The Biblical Notion of *Kairos*

The inquiring reader will find in this thorough study in biblical
theology a discussion of questions such as these: What is the Christian definition of the virtue of prudence? What are the limits and
the advantages of the pre-Christian idea of prudence? How does
prudence relate to the real? To love? What does *kairos* mean in the
Bible? How does *kairos* relate prudence to the Spirit? To Jesus
Christ? To the announcement of salvation? To the Paschal mystery?
In what sense is the urgency of decision for Christ related to *kairos*
and prudence? How does the morality of *kairos* exclude a man-
centered perspective? How is the morality of *kairos* different from
a false situation-ethics? Is the morality of *kairos* related to community salvation? To social change? To pastoral zeal? How does
prudence in terms of *kairos* motivate pastoral sociology?

*Father Bernard Häring is a professor at the Lateran University in
Rome. Among his many books, the best known are The Law of
Christ and Christian Renewal in a Changing World.*

Translation by Rev. Philip G. Roets for *Magister,* the newsletter of the
Society of Catholic College Teachers of Sacred Doctrine. The original appeared
in *Sciences Ecclésiastiques* (Montreal), 16 (May–September 1964). The translation is reprinted here with permission.

The whole of theology in the Church is in the process of self-renewal today under the inspiration of Sacred Scripture and the Liturgy. As a result the historic-salvific structure of Christian existence is brought out in a more precise way, showing that the life of the Church and of the authentic Christian does not progress in a less dynamic fashion than modern society which is so dynamic.

The state of tension of the Christian living in the old *aion* (radically passed away, but to the pressure of which we are always subject) and at the same time received into the new *aion* (completely gratuitous) which is the hour of salvation through Christ, is expressed among other ways in the theological virtue of hope. Unfortunately, in the current manuals which are the moral theology of the last two centuries, the riches of community salvation and the salvific history of hope have not been sufficiently brought out. The same is true of the virtue of prudence: prudence is the art of adapting action to the action of Christ for the redemption of the world within the whole history of salvation and within a present salvific community.

It seems to me that the biblical notion or better the biblical theology of *kairos* and the expression of *hora*, particularly dear to John, has an incalculable fertility for the renewal of moral theology in the perspective of salvation history and especially for the treatise on the virtue of prudence. On this score we are not treating merely of working out an examination of conscience for moral theology in general, but also of determining the theological meaning of pastoral sociology considered as an instrument of prudence oriented toward the historic and community perspective of salvation.

Prudence as Attention to the *Kairos*

In the ethics of Aristotle, strongly oriented toward political and civic action, just as in the moral philosophy of stoicism, always attentive to the soul of the universe which penetrates all things, the virtue of prudence plays a decisive role. But in spite of these points of social contact, these philosophies have given prudence a function that is very clearly anthropocentric: it is concerned always in the first place with the perfection of man and his search for happiness. On the other hand, the fact that they gave the virtue of prudence a central place protected the ethics from the capital dangers of formalism and legalism. Thus, already in the pre-Christian ethics, prudence was understood as a *sense of the real*.

For the Christian, to take reality seriously as a matter for decision and for human acting carries with it a new urgency. Does it treat of a mere application of general principles to a particular case in which nothing more is found than a reflection of the general principle? Certainly, the prudent man must observe and follow general principles and norms. However, prudence discovers *more* than isolated applications of the general notion and general demands of the essence. It explores of the inexhaustible riches of the concrete conditions of existence and it seeks in them the possibilities, limited but concretely accessible, of accomplishing the good in a meaningful and ever original way (this originality is greater or less each time according to the moral "genius" of each one). The virtue of prudence seeks an ever new way for each to answer the historic challenge and the possibilities of his existence.[1]

For Christian morality, prudence is the open eye which recognizes in the material data of reality the concrete task of the love of God and which builds into this same material the fulfillment of this task in love. Augustine had already given this function to the virtue of prudence to be the mediator of love:

> Prudence is love that is clearsighted for that which helps it and that which harms it. And we are not treating here of just any love, but of the love for God, supreme good, supreme wisdom and unity: therefore we can describe prudence as this love which knows how to distinguish between that which is favorable to it and that which is an obstacle to it on the way towards God.[2]

St. Thomas takes up the essence of these reflections when he writes: "Prudence can be called love, not essentially, but insofar as love moves to the act of prudence." [3]

Hence, both for Augustine and for Thomas, prudence is a virtue which expresses in a specific manner the "itinerant situation" of man. Christian prudence is the action of love that hopes, of love that strives with all its strength for the goal, in keeping with the demands of the real. This is something completely different from the schema of Aristotelian thought too often simplified (end and means), a schema which leads us to think rather of the worship of the mechanic (*homo faber*) rather than of the encounter of *homo sapiens* with the living reality that challenges him.

The virtue of prudence will certainly be presented in a very much more Christian manner in our moral treatises if we see it in the light of the biblical notion of *kairos*. This notion can make perceptible in a new way what several other truths of Sacred Scripture explicitly underline. The man-centeredness has come down off the pedestal, when it is recognized that prudence in its definitive stage is not the personal providence of man, nor his ability to make plans for his future, but *humble awareness* that opens out into the loving and completely wise Providence of God. It is an "eschatological virtue."

Those virgins are wise who are ready and wide awake for the coming of the husband (cf. Mt 25:4). The kingdom of the heavens demands, during the intermediary present time, vigilance and detachment at every instant: "For the Son of Man will come at a moment when you do not think" (Mt 24:44). So also Peter gives an eschatological basis to the necessity for prudence, but precisely in such a way that the orientation toward the final reality already begun influences the present salutary moment: "Be wise and attentive in prayer! The end of all things is at hand" (1 Pet 4:7).

Only the spiritual man who abandons himself "to the law of the Spirit which is life into Jesus Christ" (Rom 8:2) can truly be prudent and can understand the aspiration of creation to share in the spiritual freedom of the children of God so as to answer in this same freedom. "For the desire of the flesh is death, while the desire of the spirit is life and peace, since the desire of the flesh is the enemy of God. It is not submissive to the law of God; it cannot be."

The biblical notion of *kairos* as well as the corresponding detachment and watchfulness are expressions of the "meaning of the Spirit." What Sacred Scripture says about *kairos* clearly explains the signification of the "meaning of the Spirit" for the building up of the life of the individual and for the Christian community. Prudence, the theology of *kairos* tells us, is the attitude of the spiritual man who "recognizes the signs of the time" and who answers *yes* with a filial spirit to the salutary instant unceasingly prepared by God and to the task assigned to this instant.

Christ, the "Yes" to the *Kairos*

Qoheleth knows that everything has its time (its *kairos*). "Every thing under the heavens has its time. There is a time to be born and a time to die . . . a time for snatching up and a time for con-

structing . . . a time for embracing and a time to avoid it . . . a
time to be silent and a time to speak" (Qoh 3:1–8). But behind
this experience is a certain pessimism: "God has indeed made everything in its time. Even eternity he has placed in the heart of the
children of men; and yet man cannot understand the work that
God has done from its beginning to its end" (Qoh 3:11). Thus the
pre-Christian wise man can offer only prudent approximations. He
cannot offer the final solution which is the interaction of eternity
and the times marked by God for each action. This is the situation
of man waiting for the fullness of times, in the light of which the
meaning of each time prepared by God will become clear.

It is not the least important part of the message of the joy of
Jesus to proclaim the bursting forth of the time of salvation, which
reveals to men their fullness and invites them thus to a clear and full
decision. The primitive Gospel—the summary of the preaching of
Jesus in Mark—begins with this announcement that now the "kairos,
the time of salvation which enlightens and challenges men with
power, is at hand." After John has been handed over, Jesus returns
to Galilee. The Good News comes from God, he there proclaims in
these terms: "The times are fulfilled and the Kingdom of God is at
hand: be totally dedicated and amen the Good News" (Mk 1:14).
In Jesus has come the kairos, the time of salvation par excellence
predetermined and prepared for by God.

Christ himself is the bearer of the kairos in his first coming and
he fulfills it in his second coming. But he is also the prototype who
teaches us how we must conduct ourselves in regard to the kairos.

In Christ the kairos comes: "At the appointed times, God revealed
his word (his Logos)" (Tit 1:3), his revelation which continues
in the proclamation of the apostles, in the time of salvation appointed by God (cf. 1 Tim 2:6). "In his own time—on that day
which the Blessed and Unique Sovereign, the King of Kings and
Lord of Lords, will cause to appear at the appointed times" (1 Tim
6:15). This text stresses from the start the sovereignty of God who
determines his times. "When we were still in misery, Christ, at the
set time, died for those who were separated from God" (Rom 5:6).
Jesus stresses that it is the Father in his absolute sovereignty who
has determined the moments of salvation (Ac 1:7). By declaring
on many occasions, as a fact, that his action is entirely directed
according to the times of salvation determined by the Father, he
makes it clear that in him the Kingdom of God has come: he allows

himself to be led entirely by the will of the Father which is expressed in the *kairos*. He does not himself establish the plan of his life, but he accepts the salutary moment in its concrete structure with obedience and confidence in regard to the Father. His gaze is fixed on the will of the Father which grants to him to act and reveal himself (*kairois hidiois*) at the determined, favorable time. And everything that the Lord does, he does "in that time" (*en ekeinoi toi kairoi*), in the salutary moment predetermined each time by the Father. This is specially brought out in the particularly important moments of the life of Jesus, for example, at the time of the revelation of the name of God the Father, in the thanksgiving for the revelation to the totally dedicated: "I praise you, Father, Lord of heaven and earth" (Mt 11:25).

Jesus is the absolute prototype of his disciples in his attitude toward the Father. He is turned entirely toward the Father, in order to receive the *kairos* from him with obedience. He expressly contrasts his attitude toward the *kairos* to that of his unbelieving relatives: "My time has not yet come. Your time is always ready. Go to the feast. I am not going because my time is not yet fulfilled" (Jn 7:6–8). Those around Jesus, who are practically without faith, decide for themselves. They determine their own plans and their own time. Even when treating, according to the Law and prescription, of going to the feasts and making pilgrimages, it is still more their own plan than the consideration of the will of God which is at work. Jesus does not map out his plan of life in an autonomous fashion, but he welcomes his life with its salutary moments from the hands of the Father. In this he fulfills the prophecy of the Servant of Yahweh: "The Lord opens my ear each morning, in order that I may listen to him as a disciple. The Lord God has opened my ear. And I did not resist, I did not turn my back" (Is 50:4–5).

Jesus sees the different moments of his action during his life always in the light of his Hour par excellence (*hora*, especially in St. John, in a sense very close to *kairos*). The hour of his death and his glorification illumines with its light all the other situations of his life, and in such a way that in it likewise are manifest the decision of the love of the Father and the fullness of the salvific action. At the wedding feast in Cana, the Lord answers his mother: "My Hour has not yet come" (Jn 2:4).

Thus the great moment in which Jesus begins his signs and the revelation of his glory (Jn 2:11) is from the start entirely placed in the magnetic field and within the radiation of the great Hour which is the turning point in the history of the world, the Hour of the establishment of the Covenant in his blood, of the revelation of his glory in the Paschal mystery. The account of the washing of the feet and of the other events which unfold in the Supper Room is dominated by the precise declaration: "Because Jesus knew that his *kairos* had come to go back to his Father" (Jn 13:1; cf. Lk 22:14: "As the hour had come"). Already to the proprietor of the Supper Room, he sent them to say: "My time is at hand. I wish to observe in your house the feast of the Passover with my disciples" (Mt 26:18). Jesus recognizes and feels in all its depth and fullness the great hour of salvation: 'After these words, Jesus raised his eyes to heaven and said: 'My Father, the hour has come, glorify your Son in order that your Son may glorify you'" (Jn 17:1). He knows beforehand the terrible anguish and the weight of decision which his hour is bringing and at the same time he answers with a *Yes* full of abandon to the moment prepared by the Father, conscious of its height and depth and length and breadth: "What shall I say? Father, deliver me from this hour? It is for this hour that I have come. Father, glorify your name" (Jn 12:27f.). Jesus sees his own life completely oriented toward this hour. He sees also how this hour becomes an hour of salvation for all, including the pagans. When some Greeks ask to see him, he makes this prayer: "The hour has come in which the Son of Man is glorified. Amen I say to you, unless the grain of wheat fall into the ground and die, it remains alone. But if it die, it brings forth much fruit" (Jn 12:23f.).

The Morality of Imitation Under the Sign of *Kairos*

Starting with the primitive Gospel (Mk 1:14f.), from the first sermon of Jesus, which can be considered as an essential synthesis of his entire message, it is quite clear that the Christian life is under the sign of *kairos*, which must be acknowledged and accepted with gratitude. From the message of joy which is "The *kairos* is fulfilled," flows the religious demand and the decisive ethic: "Be totally dedicated and amen the message which is joy" (Mk 1:15).

And it is like a commentary on the primitive Gospel that Paul is making when he deduces the following lofty ethical demands from the fact that the *kairos* is at hand and is imminent: that married Christians are to be as unattached in the Lord in marriage as celibates, that those who weep and suffer lift themselves up in a joyous faith beyond their situation to the *kairos*, that those for whom everything succeeds do not forget the time of decision, that those who have a profession in the world bear witness in this also that the time of salvation is fulfilled and urgent (1 Cor 7:29f.). St. Peter also in his appeal to conversion refers to this fact that the *kairos* is present (Ac 3:19f.). Even more in the discourse of Paul this bond between *kairos* and conversion is clearly pointed out: "At the perfectly fitting time I heard you and in the time of salvation I helped you. Behold, the time desired has arrived; behold, the time of salvation has come" (2 Cor 6:2). In the final analysis, the morality of *kairos* is nothing other than the Law of Grace. The Apostle, who considers his own apostolic vocation as a humble *collaboration* in the divine salvific action of God, thus exhorts in this context: "Do not receive the grace of God in vain" (2 Cor 6:1). This means that the fullness of grace of this time of salvation must be our decisive norm. In the same context, he speaks again of vigilance born of zeal for souls, which takes care not to give scandal in any way (2 Cor 6:3).

Kairos is the time of the coming of the Lord, of his first coming which reaches its peak in the Paschal Mystery of the death and Resurrection of Christ, and also of his second coming. These salutary events are like the guiding stars of the Christian life. They touch the individual in a very concrete way and form him on the model, Jesus, with the same attitude of welcome acceptance in regard to the hours of salvation determined by God. This transformation is effected very specially by the sacraments. The institution of the Eucharist in the Supper Room belongs in a very special way to the *hour*, to the *kairos* of Jesus and his disciples. Thus in the Eucharist we become the contemporaries of Christ, not by virtue of the time which comes to an end, i.e., *chronos*, but according to the time of grace. Hence we are not placed in just any moment of grace or before just any urgent appeal or call, but in the very hour of salvation itself, in the fullness of salvation and before the pressing demand of the *kairos* of Christ, of his first and of his second coming. These are the two moments which demand of us a serious decision. The Christian, who by his baptism is integrated into the salvific events of the death and the resurrection of Christ and who in the Eucharist "proclaims the death of the Lord, until he comes" (1 Cor

11:26), can and must consider the divine appeal in his present
situation of decision as an effect in him of the great salvific hours
of Christ.

> Thus the Greek notion of *kairos* formulates for us with a sharp-
> ness that is no longer familiar to our religious thought the seriousness
> of the decision before which we are placed by Jesus in the proclama-
> tion of his religious message and by Paul in his moral demands: the
> more the end becomes visible in the fulfillment already present, the
> stronger becomes the demand of the *kairos,* a demand renewed at
> each instant of Christian existence, and which by this very persistence
> demands of the Christian that he be unceasingly conscious of the
> *kairos* itself and that he be faithful to it in its concrete demands, for
> example, in the manifestation of fraternal love (Rom 13:8–11).[4]

To walk in the footsteps of Christ in adherence to the *kairos* continually renewed means a personal adherence to God in Christ
Jesus, expressed by an unreserved disposition to vigilance and obedience regarding his invitation of grace and by a loving consideration
for the needs of the neighbor and the community. This perspective
is clearly revealed, for example, in the warning of our Lord concerning the salvific moment of his return and the fearful judgment
that will precede it: "At every moment (*en panti kairo*) be attentive to prayer so that you be prepared for what must happen and
for the meeting with the Son of Man" (Lk 21:36). The great salvific
event of the Return is already really an act in each Christian existence, and demands in grace and power a constant vigilance with
regard to all occasions, with regard to each gift of grace and each
moment of decision. The same perspective is drawn from analogous
exhortations: "Pray unceasingly, watch and pray; for you do not
know when the *kairos* is coming. . . . Pay attention; for you do not
know when the Lord will come, so that when he does come, he does
not find you sleeping. I say to all of you: be vigilant" (Mk 13:33–37;
cf. Lk 12:40).

This entire time of salvation between the first and the second
coming of Christ forms "the last hour" (1 Jn 2:18) and, as such, is
placed under the sign of absolute vigilance with regard to the
salvific plans of God, which do not permit man to make his own plan
for himself. This hour of salvation, threatened and threatening, demands a constant conversion. And it is lukewarmness or indifference
above all that it strikes against: "And this is important for us who
understand the time of salvation (the *kairos*): now is the hour to
awaken from our sleep" (Rom 13:11).

The very hour of temptation is for the believer a *kairos* (cf. Lk 8:13; the *kairos* of temptation; Apoc 3:10: the hour of temptation). This *kairos* must, according to the plan of God's love, awaken the believer from his sleepiness and shake off his indifference, lead him to prayer and guide him in grace to the radical choice of good. The Lord is then ready to deliver his own from the hour of temptation.

And all those who, in the light of the fullness of salvation of the *kairos*, leave everything to adhere to the hour without swerving will receive at that time a hundredfold both in joys and in sufferings. This means that the *kairos* offers them hundredfold opportunities to deepen and render perfect their choice of the Lord (cf. Mk 10:29–31).

Each hour of decision, each *kairos* determined by the Lord carries in itself the eschatological fullness and the power of the judgment; each is attached to the great and final hour of the separation of the good and the evil and of the judgment (cf. Apoc 14:7). The final hour, the hour of judgment, is thus in an entirely special way for the disciples of Jesus an hour of fulfillment, because they have already pledged themselves for him (cf. Apoc 14:15).

If then we consider that each hour impels to a sincere decision in the light of the great events of salvation, we are no longer surprised to hear the apostle Peter state, in reference to the *kairos*, that "the judgment begins in the house of God" (1 Pet 4:17). On the one hand the *kairos* is a punishment of the house of God because Christians do not fully live according to the fullness of grace of the last times; on the other hand, the trial is a grace from the long-suffering God who unceasingly invites his own with such an urgency to renunciation and full conversion. For those who refuse the faith, the *kairos* of judgment in the house of God is a terrible warning: "If in fact the judgment is beginning with us, what will be the end of those who do not obey the Gospel?" (1 Pet 4:17).

The morality of *kairos* excludes all autonomous planning on the part of man. It is also at the opposite end from the Aristotelian anthropocentric category which ranges everything in the perspective of the goal (happiness of the individual) and of the means (useful, possible, or necessary for this goal), a perspective from which we come quite frequently to the conclusion that we are not bound to respond to these graces prepared by God because they do not represent any necessary means for the attainment of beatitude. In fact, in this perspective they can simply give up the merit which the use of these graces would procure. The morality of the Gospel, on the contrary, demands above all vigilance and absolute self-detachment in regard to the concrete possibility of good which God has prepared for each particular hour.

Not to make any autonomous plan does not mean in any sense to develop a tendency to quietism. Just the opposite. The ethics of *kairos* is incomparably dynamic, demanding, for it is from God himself that it receives its active power. In the broad context of the Letter to the Galatians, for example, the reference to *kairos* is a new aspect which stresses more than once that the morality of the freedom of the children of God is neither the absence of law nor arbitrariness, nor above all, sloth: "Let us do good untiringly. If we are not negligent, we shall harvest the fruits in the *kairos*. Hence in the measure in which the *kairos* permits us, let us do good perfectly toward all but especially toward our brothers in the faith" (Gal 6:9). And this exhortation comes up again, although in different expressions, in the Letter to the Ephesians and to the Colossians: "Redeem the entire *kairos;* for the times are evil" (Eph 5:16). For him who does not exhaust the always renewed *kairos,* the possibilities of each present hour do not come back; for him the times are truly bad. In the Letter to the Colossians, as well as in Galatians, this characteristic of *kairos,* i.e., its being the unique occasion for apostolic efficacy, comes back in the form of a salutary hour of fraternal love: "Act wisely toward those from the outside by profiting from the *kairos*" (Col 4:5).

These high demands of *kairos* are accessible to the Christian in relation to Christ and through the Spirit sent by him.

The Morality of *Kairos* and the False Situation-Ethics

A person who does not know Christian morality except from the outside may perhaps ask whether this perspective (of morality), starting from the hour of salvation, is not too close to this false situation-morality which the Church has been obliged to condemn several times in recent years. Hence would it not be safer, in reaction against situation-ethics, to stress more the precise frontiers or limits of permissions and prohibitions, without stressing the *kairos?* The answer to this is that the first problem of the Christian and theologian is not to be what is the surest but what expresses the Word of God in the most faithful way possible. Undoubtedly, we must clearly and firmly state the limits of the lawful. There are certain minimal demands, clear and obligatory on all, coming at the same time from natural law and the present economy of salvation. But it would be absolutely unfaithful to the time of the fullness of salvation to wish to put the stress solely on these minimal demands. The basic formula of the new Law, "the law of the Spirit of life into Christ Jesus," is the great commandment which obliges us to strive unceasingly toward a more perfect love of God and the neighbor. The peak of the Sermon on the Mount is: "Be perfect as your heavenly Father is perfect" (Mt 5:48). Moreover, there is no doubt, in the intention of the Evangelist, an intention expressed here with unsurpassable clarity, that the Sermon on the Mount is the proclamation of the new Law, which obliges each person, and this in the form of commandments of striving, in the form of daily obligatory effort, in the rhythm of grace proportionately given.

Moreover, it is important to add that a morality which one-sidedly draws the attention of Christians to the strict limits of general demands has a fatal tendency to draw dangerously near to a false situation-ethics, and places the weak in the immediate danger of not going one single step beyond these limits. For a one-sided morality attached to minimal demands psychologically attracts men to these limits, just as a fence line in a pasture almost fatally attracts the animals to pasture near it even if this is an electric fence. Secondly, the one-sided morality of "fences" has presented the demands of the natural law and the Gospel as simple basic requisites demanded by the positive law and, frequently also, has not clearly distinguished between the domain of each, thus stirring up the reaction of the false situation-morality.

To speak positively, we must therefore insist first on this fact that the biblical morality of *kairos* is actually the most radical opposite of false situation-ethics and that it alone can restore all morality. Moreover, the principal differences between the morality of *kairos* and situation-morality are the following:

1. A complete difference in *orientation:* situation-ethics strives to stress human freedom, the spirit of initiative and autonomous realization of the person beyond the limits of the essential order willed by the Creator and the Savior. It pastures entirely outside the fence. The ethics of *kairos*, on the contrary, is constantly and energetically on the march toward a point opposite to the minimal limit and in the direction, without compromise of the central domain,

which is the perfect love of God and the neighbor, in a growing
fidelity to the demands of all the virtues understood in the final
analysis as mediators of love of God and of neighbor.

2. The false situation-ethics is an expression of the *sarx*, of the
selfish man, bound to his ego, for whom the only thing that counts
in the end is his own glory, the declaration of his own liberty and,
at best, a personal perfection, poorly understood. The ethics of
kairos, on the contrary, is a gift and a realization of the *Pneuma*, the
Spirit of Christ. It is the ethics of the spiritual man, of the man who
precisely is no longer under the law insofar as he permits himself to
be led by the Spirit (Gal 5:18; Rom 6:14; 8:14), not just by attaining the limit of the law nor by accepting it as a mere minimal demand nor as a burden imposed from outside. The man of the *sarx*,
the man who arranges his life in an autonomous fashion, does not
know how to subordinate himself to the minimal demands of the
law imposed from the outside (cf. Rom 8:3) and even less to the
law, a source of life, which is grace. But the Christian, the spiritual
man, who makes the most of the *kairos*, fulfills the minimal demands
in this that he goes beyond them constantly, in this that he does not
look directly to the fulfilling of them but turns his gaze toward the
purpose of the law, love of Christ, and strives directly for this objective.

3. The situation-ethics of existentialism wrongly understood is
individualistic. The ethics of the *kairos*, on the contrary, is essentially attached to the community salvation. Precisely in the salvific
solidarity given by Christ, each individual and each community
fulfills his own *kairos*, his own capabilities for "the upbuilding of
the Body which is Christ" (cf. Eph 4; 1 Cor 12).

The Socio-Salvific Dimensions of *Kairos*

The time of grace, the hour unceasingly prepared by God with
all its irreversible possibilities, is clearly addressed to each one personally, but summons or challenges each in his personal responsibility before the community. As we have already remarked, the
kairos which the Christian must "redeem" means his participation
in the *kairos* of Christ and thus on this title is a mission toward the
community (cf. Col 4:5). And not only this: the *kairos* can also
summon or challenge the community immediately, or, in other
words, the community itself is also subject to the biblical morality

of the *kairos*. The *kairos* of Christ, new head of mankind, is the time of salvation for the entire family of the redeemed. And consequently his chosen people also have his *kairos* in that which concerns his coming, his preaching, and his manifestations of power.

The Lord weeps over Jerusalem because it "did not know the *kairos* of his visit" (Lk 19:44). Jesus reproaches the crowds for knowing how to observe the earthly signs of the times and their corresponding actions, but not knowing how to examine when they should the signs announcing the time of salvation which has come. "You hypocrites, you know how to evaluate the face of the heavens and the earth; how does it happen that you cannot judge the signs of the *kairos?*" (Lk 12:57). In Mt 16:1ff., the same reproach is addressed in a very special way to the leaders of the people, to the Pharisees and the Sadducees. They, above all, should have recognized, according to the signs accomplished by Jesus, according to his testimony and personality, that already the great time of salvation had begun.

Kairos and the Sociological Situation

Sociology or the social sciences study social facts and certain recurring tendencies. They look for a science of change and pattern of the interdependencies between religion and the social factors. Now one of the characteristics of sociology is to seek the sociological causes. This introduces into sociology here and there a typically determinist note. The sociological situation is then considered up to a certain point as a fatality, even though today the summary "sociologism," which intends to explain everything by starting with sociological factors as inexorable quantities, is clearly on the decline. At any rate, such a sociology seems to have nothing in common with the biblical conception of *kairos*.

However, an unprejudiced sociology can today clearly show us that the quasi-quantities and determinisms that can be uncovered are actually to a great extent the consequences of freedom, of freedom pledged in this or that way, or even insufficiently pledged by the individual, or by groups, or by society itself.

Sociology, together with psychology, destroys several illusions of absolute arbitrary freedom. But it helps also to uncover the authentic possibilities which the individual and society constantly have for taking the next step toward a greater freedom in the direction of good. It especially helps us to see that without the solidary pledge of freedom and without an investment of freedom put to work in a solidary fashion in the economic and social structures and in the culture and life of the mind, individual freedom becomes more and more captive. These notions are set completely in the line of the biblical notion of *kairos*. Man cannot pretend that he can realize good in an ahistoric manner by choosing each time in an autonomous way between the thousands of possibilities. Rather he must humbly explore the possibilities, limited, modest, but real. And in the measure that he receives them, new doors are constantly opened before him toward unsuspected possibilities of progress in freedom and good.

Pastoral Sociology and the "Sign of the Times"

Bringing out the theological value of the biblical doctrine of *kairos* forms one of the necessary bases for a productive understanding of pastoral sociology. Only in this perspective is it significant for the moralist and for the shepherd of souls to study the sociological bases of Catholic moral theology.

We do not intend to say, however, that the doctrine of *kairos* alone can suffice to establish a theological introduction or a practical introduction to the usage adapted by empiric sociology in a constructive pastoral theology. For the study of other great socio-salvific perspectives is almost as indispensable: consider the mystery of the Incarnation and the *incarnate* character of the Christian religion, the relations of the universe and the kingdom of God, the salvific solidarity of all men in Adam and even more in Christ, the biblical notion of the person with its basic existential categories—*I, You, We,* and so on.

The Second Vatican Council is placed, on the one hand, under the sign of the greatest mystery of the Christian religion, the mystery of unity which has its permanent root in the mystery of the Trinity and which returns to it, and on the other hand, *under the sign of the Kairos.* The opening discourse of Pope John XXIII at the time of the first session clearly shows the setting of the Council. The Council must—this is the clear directive of the Pope of the Council—seek to know the signs of the times. And this brings with it also the study of the form of the spirit and the form of the thought of men of today. Their needs and the special ways by which we can reach them must be respected by him who presents the message of salvation. Only thus the Church can continue to proclaim the Word of God in a way fitted to the time: this means both in the language of men of a time and in absolute fidelity to him who has come from heaven to us. The thought of the Council, moreover, is strongly marked by the experience of unity in diversity and diversity in unity. Already the constitution on the renewal of the liturgy clearly states that the Church must study, within each culture and each period, the form of spirit and forms of expression of men in order to render accessible to them the riches of the liturgy and to lead them to share in community in the gladness of celebration and in the faithful fulfillment of the liturgical function.

At a great turning point of history, the Church of the Second Vatican Council considers with an impartial love, in an authentic spirit of Catholicity, the different cultures in which the Church itself, its doctrine, its morality, its liturgy, its pastoral love must become flesh and blood. In the meeting of so many different cultures within one and the same Church, it becomes very much more evident that man is essentially an historic being and therefore to act in conformity with history is not something added in an accessory manner to the general demands of the *lex naturae*, of the natural moral law. Rather, to act in conformity with history constitutes one of the constant demands of human nature, of acting as a human being, and of authentic fidelity to the vocation of man.

Pastoral sociology is a necessity in a world which changes with almost blinding speed, to which we cannot bring the Gospel and in which we cannot establish the Christian religion unless we keep our hand constantly on the pulse of the life leaping through. Thus it is exact to say that pastoral sociology has its *kairos* today, that it is necessary if we wish to recognize and to use to the full the present *kairos*. In a closed society, unanimous and static, pastoral sociology could be bypassed. The wisdom of men and women advanced in age would be enough. But in an age of such vehement passage to forms of life entirely new in a pluralist society with extreme differences, open on every side and dynamic, pastoral sociology cannot bypass these instruments which are indispensable to the life of our times. Experimental sociology is one of these instruments. It contributes to an objective evaluation of the many-sided exchanges which are effected between religion, the moral and religious life of individuals and society, and the factors of the surrounding world, the sociological, economic, cultural, and political forces. It explores the mentality of the present time, seeking to learn how it is revealed in the different moral and religious problems and the manner in which it can be brought face to face with the truth and absolute moral demands. It tracks down the causes of new difficulties and points out new possibilities. It is important to note here, nevertheless, that empiric sociology alone is incapable of formulating the "signs of the times" in terms of *kairos*. Experience alone cannot be the measure of things. Pastoral sociology is then a subordinate science, like the history of the Church. It is, in the sociological sense, a science of empiric approach. It must face the facts with real serious-mindedness. For if the observation of the facts is not adequate, how could the signs of the times be interposed in a meaningful manner so as to develop into a wise pastoral plan that is close to reality? But at the same time, the interpretation of these facts is formulated ultimately in the light of theology, under the sign of faith. For the theological-pastoral situation is already in great part the object of research. And therefore only he whom faith and the gift of wisdom have made a wise man can correctly use the materials of sociological research to interpret the "signs of the times."

Hence a precise distinction between empiric sociological research and theological knowledge must be made. On the one hand we use all the human scientific means available, but on the other hand, the evaluation must be made under the inspiration of faith.

Only by adopting this attitude, imposed by the biblical doctrine of *kairos*, can we study the signs of the times, evaluate the sociological materials, and understand the possibilities and depth of decision which our time contains.

Hence only when in Christian morality the actions of the individual and communities are determined by the *kairos* can we hope that, considered as a whole, pastoral sociology and its evaluations will become the expression of a constant vigilance and open-mindedness to hear in the voice of the time of God. It will therefore be the expression of an open-mindedness to listen very attentively, very conscientiously to all the resources of research in order better to hear this voice.

The Pastoral Plan with a Socio-Pastoral Basis and the *Kairos*

The biblical notion of *kairos* forbids all autonomous making of plans, and in fact every ossifying making of plans which could turn man in any way from a constant and humble vigilance, attached to the demands of the present hour. Thus pastoral sociology would render pastoral theology a very poor service if it undertook to work out exact plans and a long-range program which would have to be carried out to the letter without any modification. Such plans are forbidden not only in historic-salvific perspective of the biblical *kairos*, but also in the sociological perspective itself. All action modifies reality. New forces which we cannot count on in advance constantly enter into play, especially the free human decision, individual and social.

Pastoral sociology can and must have its moments of maximum activity, for example, in the preparation of a regional mission. But its results can be used in an intelligent way, only if each pastor of souls and especially the director of the pastoral undertaking constantly observes the new data and the demands that arise. Then, empiric sociology will continue to help, by observing the significant traits of change. For the pastor of souls this will mean open-mindedness in accepting in a spirit of broad collaboration the general statements of the socio-pastoral research and their pastoral interpretation, and then a constant vigilance on his part to bring into harmony with these statements the new possibilities that open up, so as to join to the plan his own initiative in a spirit of solidarity. Also, the community of pastors under the guidance of the bishop or the assembly of bishops must show a constant open-mindedness in modifying the pastoral plan as a whole which corresponds to the basic structures of the period, insofar as there are new observations and new developments. Thus is united in pastoral theology the continuity and capacity for adaptation, the eternal and the demands of time, fidelity to essential common demands and fidelity to duty imposed by the historic moment.

References

1 *Summa Theol.* II–II, 47, 3.
2 Augustine, *De Moribus Ecclesiae Catholicae*, P.L. 32, 1322.
3 *Summa Theol.* II–II, 47, 1, ad 1.
4 Delling, art. "Kairos" in *TWNT*, 3, 461.

X. LOVE

The Word of God

Beloved, let us love one another, for love is from God. And everyone who loves is born of God, and knows God. He who does not love does not know God; for God is love. In this has the love of God been shown in our case that God has sent his only-begotten Son into the world that we may live through him. In this is the love, not that we have loved God, but that he has first loved us, and sent his Son a propitiation for our sins. Beloved, if God has so loved us, we also ought to love one another.

No one has ever seen God. If we love one another, God abides in us and his love is perfected in us. In this we know that we abide in him and he in us, because he has given us of his Spirit. And we have seen, and do testify, that the Father has sent his Son to be Savior of the world. Whoever confesses that Jesus is the Son of God, God abides in him and he in God. And we have come to know, and have believed, the love that God has in our behalf. God is love, and he who abides in love abides in God, and God in him.

In this is love perfected with us, that we may have confidence in the day of judgment; because as he is, even so are we also in this world. There is no fear in love; but perfect love casts out fear, because fear brings punishment. And he who fears is not perfected in love. Let us therefore love, because God first loved us. If anyone says, "I love God," and hates his brother, he is a liar. For how can he who does not love his brother, whom he sees, love God, whom he does not see? And this commandment we have from him, that he who loves God should love his brother also.

Everyone who believes that Jesus is the Christ is born of God. And everyone who loves him who begot, loves also the one begot-

ten of him. In this we know that we love the children of God, when
we love God and do his commandments. For this is the love of
God, that we keep his commandments; and his commandments are
not burdensome. Because all that is born of God overcomes the
world; and this is the victory that overcomes the world, our faith.
Who is there that overcomes the world if not he who believes that
Jesus is the Son of God?

(1 John 4:7–5:5)

KATHRYN SULLIVAN, R.S.C.J.

The God of Love

The joyful reader will discover in the positive outlook of these excerpts a discussion of questions such as these: How did the people
of the Old Testament get an insight into God's love? What images
are used to express God's love for Israel? How did this transform
Israel's understanding of the nature of sin? How do Jeremia and
Ezechiel relate this to the new messianic covenant? How then do
we explain the hatred and violence depicted in the Old Testament?
What does St. Thomas mean when he says that hatred is rooted
in love? How do we explain the jealousy of the pagan gods in ancient mythologies? What led the Old Testament writers to apply
this to Yahweh? How did Job face this mystery? How does God's
love give meaning to human existence?

Mother Kathryn Sullivan is professor of Sacred Scripture at Man-
hattanville College of the Sacred Heart. She is coauthor of *The
Catholic Biblical Encyclopedia* and editor of *The Bible Today.*

Excerpts from "The God of Israel, God of Love," reproduced with the permission of the Institute of Judaeo-Christian Studies from Volume IV (1962) of
its Yearbook, *The Bridge,* edited by John M. Oesterreicher, published by
Herder & Herder, New York.

The Voice of the Prophets

With the prophets, even before the exile and the return under Ezra, the long instruction of the chosen people entered its most important phase. Divine love had been found true by patriarchs, by wanderers in the wilderness, by pioneers in Palestine, by members of the first amphictyonies; it was found true by citizens of a unified kingdom, by brothers dwelling in a land divided, by exiles heartsick beside foreign shores, as it was to be later by the chastened members of the second commonwealth. Time had not only proved God's faithfulness, it had also disclosed new dimensions in the covenantal bond. The *anawim*, the poor of Yahweh, who in their "poverty" of soul depended on no one but him, were quick to discover these new values and the basis of a life of poverty and prayer. Having nothing, they turned with childlike confidence to him who possessed all. They never ignored or denied the juridical aspects of the covenant but they looked beyond the sign to the reality signified. They gave trust and received mercy. Their misery was an additional reason to hope in him.[1]

The experience of this mercy and well-placed hope led to a deeper insight into God's love, which the prophets sought to express in new images. Hosea describes the bond uniting Israel to her God under the figure of marriage; the words he uses have covenantal overtones:

> So I will allure her;
>   I will lead her into the desert
>   and speak to her heart. . . .
> She shall respond there as in the days of her youth,
>   when she came up from the land of Egypt.
> On that day, says the Lord,
>   she shall call me "My husband.". . .
>
>   (Hos 2:16–18)

Because of his covenant with Israel, God, like a faithful husband, will have pity on her who is unpitied, the prophet explains; he will again say to the Israelites: "My people!" and Israel shall answer "My God!" (2:23–24). No image, not even that of wedded love, is enough to describe God's bond with his people. Hence Hosea recalls a father's embrace of his son:

> Yet it was I who taught Ephraim to walk,
>   who took them in my arms;

> I drew them with human cords,
> with bands of love. . . .
>
> (Hos 11:3–4)

The book of Deuteronomy made clear that the covenant laws were neither the impositions of an exacting ruler nor the price grudgingly paid by a people needing protection; obedience to them was the grateful expression of love offered in return for multiplied proofs of the Lord's love.

> For love of your fathers he chose their descendants and personally led you out of Egypt by his great power, driving out of your way nations greater and mightier than you, so as to bring you in and to make their land your heritage, as it is today. This is why you must now know, and fix in your heart, that the Lord is God in the heavens above and on earth below, and that there is no other. You must keep his statutes and commandments which I enjoin on you today. . . .
>
> (Dt 4:37–40)

Such teaching transformed Israel's grasp of the nature of sin. It was more than an offense; it was a betrayal. It was more than the infringement of a precept; it was a failure to respond to an invitation of love. The Deuteronomist's teaching also opened the eyes of the people to the true nature of punishment. Frequently chastised for their waywardness and made subject to their enemies because of their infidelities, the people learned that to break the bond of love was to bring down suffering upon itself.

No one understood sin and punishment more clearly or explained them more poignantly than Jeremiah, and no one saw with greater vision that faithful observance of the covenant he knew pointed to a greater covenant of the future.

> The days are coming, says the Lord, when I will make a new covenant with the house of Israel and the house of Judah. It will not be like the covenant I made with their fathers the day I took them by the hand to lead them forth from the land of Egypt. . . . I will place my law within them, and write it upon their hearts; I will be their God, and they shall be my people.
>
> (Jer 31:31–33)

Loving service, freely given, will make obedience to the new covenant an unreserved donation of self.

Ezekiel, too, uses several images to hail God's pledge. God's love is as tender as a bridegroom's for his bride (see 16:8–14), as solicitous as a shepherd's for his flock: "I will appoint one shepherd over them to pasture them, my servant David. . . . I will make a covenant of peace with them. . . . Thus they shall know that I, the Lord, am their God, and they are my people, the house of Israel, says the Lord God" (34:23, 25, 30).

The Shepherd-to-come is David, another David, one who will accomplish the messianic mission promised to the king. His work will be one of peace. Thus the Second Isaiah speaks of the days of the Messiah as an era of unalloyed happiness, a fulfillment of the pledge of love:

> Though the mountains leave their place
>   and the hills be shaken,
> My love shall never leave you
>   nor my covenant of peace be shaken,
>   says the Lord, who has mercy on you. . . .
> Come to me heedfully,
>   listen, that you may have life.
> I will renew with you the everlasting covenant,
>   the benefits assured to David.
>
> (Is 54:10; 55:3)

The Mystery of Wrath

Love, it is true, is expressed in many ways in the Old Testament, but is it not equally true that the God of mercy is called the God of wrath? Can we ignore the fact that hate and violence are engraved upon its pages? Canaanites, Ammonites, Moabites, Amalekites were hostile to the descendants of Abraham; were not the descendants of Abraham hostile in their turn? More surprising, perhaps, is the hatred and violence of the just man. No doubt, a partial answer to this bewildering fact is that Israel's enemies were God's enemies. When they invaded Israel they were invading the inheritance given her by God, they were profaning his Temple, which he had chosen for his worship. It may be said that the violent outbursts of the just man against the sinners reflected his deep friendship for God. Yet, whatever explanations we try to find for man's conduct in the Old Testament, it is far harder to explain the unexpected manifestations of divine anger.

Is God the God of wrath or of love? Is he a father or a tyrant? And if he is a father, why does he make so many demands upon his children, and why does he allow so many horrors in the world he has fashioned for those whom he has called the children of his love?

"Conflict, like love, is engraved in our deepest being." [2] Hatred, sadness, despair, fear, anger—according to St. Thomas they are all rooted in love. Hatred owes its origin to the avoidance of evil, and evil is anything that is opposed to the object of our love. Sadness arises when the person or thing we love seems to elude us. Despair grips us when they seem beyond our grasp forever. Fear seizes us when the beloved is in danger; anger, when our struggle for his favor is frustrated, when our pleas are ignored and our gifts cast aside.[3]

To answer the questions, whether the God of Israel is the God of wrath or of love and how man's suffering can be reconciled to God's goodness, it is necessary to reject the alleged tensions on which they are based. There can never be any conflict between divine love and divine severity: love must always be opposed to what is contrary to love. Nor can there be any conflict between divine love and divine power: love must always employ all the resources at its command to protect what it holds dear. The biblical examples of divine jealousy and divine wrath are not the clumsy anthropomorphisms of a primitive people but the best, though not the only, means of solving the difficult problem of translating into human language something of the incommunicable realities of God's wisdom and holiness.

The jealous anger of pagan gods and goddesses is a disturbingly frequent theme of ancient mythologies. Passionate reprisals fall from the heavens with lightninglike destructiveness when these volatile and vindictive beings are aroused, or their loves are thwarted or their possessions jeopardized. Most disturbing is the appearance of such passion in Old Testament allusions to Yahweh. More surprising still is the clearly stated fact that in Yahweh love and jealousy are linked. Men who offered him a love divided would long rue their folly, but a single love would receive a lavish reward:

> You shall not carve idols for yourselves in the shape of anything in the sky above or on the earth below or in the waters beneath the earth; you shall not bow down before them or worship them. For I, the Lord, your God, am a jealous God, inflicting punishment for their fathers' wickedness on the children of those who hate me, down to the third and fourth generation; but bestowing mercy down to the thousandth generation, on the children of those who love me and keep my commandments.

> (Ex 20:4–6)

In a narrative rich in covenant traditions, Joshua reminded his contemporaries of Yahweh's goodness in times past and times more recent, of his goodness to their fathers of old and to their immediate forebears. And in it he warned them of the nature of the Lord to whom they wished to pledge their service.[4] "You may not be able," he cautioned, "to serve the Lord, for he is a holy God; he is a jealous God who will not forgive your transgressions or your sins. If, after the good he has done for you, you forsake the Lord and serve strange gods, he will do evil to you and destroy you" (24:19–20).

Joshua's fears were well founded. Prophets of the exile like Ezekiel and the Second Isaiah watched the divine jealousy become the divine wrath, saw man's sin call down upon itself the just decrees of him who is omnipotent Love.[5]

> Therefore, as I live, says the Lord God, because you have defiled my sanctuary with all your detestable abominations, I swear to cut you down. I will not look upon you with pity nor have mercy. . . . Thus shall my anger spend itself, and I will wreak my fury upon them till I am appeased; they shall know that I, the Lord, have spoken in my jealousy when I spend my fury upon them.
>
> (Ez 5:11, 13)

What is this divine wrath that is so righteously unleashed, so richly deserved, so opposed to the tolerant indifferentism of today? In biblical terms it is the manifestation of an all-holy God; it is the rejection of all that is soiling or impure; it is the punishment for sin. If we find expressions of divine anger hard to understand, so did the Jews.[6] Invariably they looked on all public calamities as signs of divine displeasure. When fire burnt the outermost part of the camp, they ignored all secondary causes and attributed the disaster to the anger of the Lord (see Nm 11:1–3). When invaders plundered the land, outwitted the slow-moving tribes, foiled their best stratagems, they ascribed their many defeats to the Lord's displeasure with his own (see Jgs 2:14–15). Conversely, good fortune and welcome success seemed the harbingers of his contentment, prosperity the proof that his anger had waned.

Puzzled, the author of the book of Job seems to plumb the depths of this mystery. He states his case plainly: The Lord is responsible, let him explain and justify his ways with the world:

> It is all one! therefore I say:
>   Both the innocent and the wicked he destroys.
> When the scourge slays suddenly,
>   He laughs at the despair of the innocent.
> The earth is given into the hands of the wicked;

> He covers the faces of its judges.
> If it is not he, who then is it?
>
> (Jb 9:22–24)

From the midst of a whirlwind Job learned his lesson. Unhesitatingly, the Lord began his queries: Where was Job when the earth was measured, when the morning stars sang together, when the sea was set behind its bars, when the dawn flung away the darkness, when man's exits and entrances were planned, when snow and hail were stored in the sky, when stars were flung jewel-like against the heavens, when birds and beasts and fish were given their domain? All this and much more was required of the man who had "clouded the truth with words ill-considered" (see 38:2) and who acknowledged that he was unable to explain all the mystery of the visible world. It is not to be wondered, then, that the mystery of the invisible world was beyond his understanding.

Were God man's equal, he might be understood; were he an "extra," a mere addition to our existence, he might be ignored. Since he is the Wholly-other, the All-powerful, the All-wise, the Sublime, the Ever-present, the Always-acting, the Eternally-immutable, the Omniscient and the Good, he must be served. In this brief day, man can do no better than honor him who is near yet totally unique, praise him without whose power he would not be, exalt him whose wisdom gives meaning to all things, revere him who is above all creatures, near all creatures, protecting all creatures, unchangingly concerned about those to whom he gives all manner of unrecognized good.

Had they encountered the God of Israel, all the sages of East and West would have found in the two Testaments the love for which they searched, which alone could satisfy their deepest needs and fulfill their most hidden desires.[7] So mighty is the love of Yahweh, so wise, so inscrutable that the sorrows of man, even his wickedness and mistakes, not to speak of his virtues and joy, have eternal meaning in the mystery of this love.

References

[1] See Albert Gelin, "Heureux les pauvres," *Grands Thèmes Bibliques*, pp. 79–83. In this short chapter all the pertinent texts concerning the *anawim* are assembled and the history of these privileged souls is skillfully summarized. Poverty which had once been a sociological problem was later recognized as a spiritual qualification. It became a synonym for piety. Jeremiah was the patron

of the *anawim*, Job the literary model of their dialogue with God. On the shores of the Dead Sea, the Qumranites tried to fashion their lives according to this teaching. On the Mount of Beatitudes, Jesus blessed and promised the poor a great reward. See also Albert Gelin, *Les pauvres de Yahvé* (Paris: Cerf, 1953); English translation by Kathryn Sullivan, R.S.C.J., *The Poor of Yahweh* (Liturgical Press, 1964).

² Philippe de la Trinité, O.C.D., "God of Wrath or God of Love?" *Love and Violence,* ed. Bruno de Jesus-Marie, O.C.D. (New York: Sheed and Ward, 1954), p. 123; see also Fidelis Buck, S.J., *Die Liebe Gottes beim Propheten Osee* (Rome: Tipografia Pio X, 1953), pp. 80–85.

³ See Philippe de la Trinité, *op. cit.,* p. 124; cf. *Summa Theol.* II–II, qq. 34, 20, 19, 37.

⁴ See George E. Mendenhall, "Covenant Forms in Israelite Tradition," *The Biblical Archaeologist,* 17 (September 1954), 50–76. This analysis of Hittite suzerainty treaties throws great light on the covenant concept of Israel and is indispensable for an understanding of Jos 24. See also Neal M. Flanagan, "The Covenant and How It Grew," *American Ecclesiastical Review,* 143 (September 1960), 145–56.

⁵ See Ez 36:5; 38:19; Is 42:13; also Ps 36:1; Prv 23:17.

⁶ See Philippe de la Trinité, *op. cit.,* p. 123.

⁷ The unique moral contribution of ancient Israel is examined by John Ferguson in *Moral Values in the Ancient World* (New York: Barnes and Noble, 1959). In his conclusion he declares that "*'ahabah,* the election-love which represents the very nature of God, when applied to man, slides over into *hesed,* the loyal fulfillment of covenanted obligations, and *hesed,* when it requires definition, is seen in terms of *zedek* which, while remaining theocentric, expresses, I think, at first at least, God's will rather than his nature" (p. 226).

THOMAS BARROSSE, C.S.C.

Some Aspects of Love and Faith in St. John

The joyful reader may conclude his happy excursions into biblical morality by pondering at last the analysis in the brief but basic excerpts that follow the discussion of questions such as these: How does the third chapter of St. John's Gospel relate faith and love? What is special about John's remark that "God loved the world"? In what sense does this love demand a response? How is faith presented as the appropriate response to God's love? What are the possible interpretations of the expression "love of God"? What then does it mean to say we have "the love of God" in us?

Father Thomas Barrosse is professor of Sacred Scripture at Holy Cross College in Washington, D.C., and the author of God Speaks to Men.

Faith Is Man's Response to God's Love

John 3:14–21 is the first detailed text which explicitly discusses faith in the fourth Gospel after the prologue. And in this very first detailed text faith stands in a context of love: it is man's response to the advances of God's love; it is opposed by love of the darkness; it is accompanied (so the implication seems to be) by love of the light.

(14) And as Moses lifted up the serpent in the desert, even so must the Son of Man be lifted up, (15) that everyone who believes in him may have life everlasting. (16) For God so loved the world that he gave his only-begotten Son, that everyone who believes in him may not perish, but may have life everlasting. (17) For God did not send

These excerpts are reprinted with permission from an article entitled "Love and Faith in St. John," *Theological Studies*, 18, 4 (December 1957).

his Son into the world in order to judge the world, but that the world might be saved through him. (18) He who believes in him is not judged; but he who does not believe has already been judged, because he has not believed in the name of the only-begotten Son of God. (19) Now this is the judgment: the light has come into the world, yet men have loved the darkness rather than the light, for their works were wicked. (20) For everyone who does evil hates the light and does not come to the light, that his deeds may not be accused, (21) but he who does the truth comes to the light that his deeds may be made manifest, for they have been performed in God.

Verse 16 is clear: God's sending his Son into the world on his salvific mission is an act of love for the world. The verb standing in the aorist presents the divine love as something past. John certainly does not mean to imply that God's salvific love has ceased or that his love no longer offers salvation to all through Christ (cf. Jn 12:44–50; 17:20, 23). But the act of love as expressed in the Son's coming into the world (the Father "gave" him) is past.

"God loved the world." The universality of God's love expressed in Christ's coming is undeniable. Christ comes not "to judge the world" but only "that the world might be saved through him" (v. 17). If anyone fails to receive the salvation offered by the Son, all responsibility lies with him and none with Christ: condemnation does not come from the Son, but those who reject him condemn themselves by rejecting their only hope of salvation (v. 18). The universality of Christ's mission implies the universality of the divine love which inspires it.

The text just considered is the sole passage in the Johannine writings which speaks of God's *love* for all men. John refers frequently to divine benevolence for men but avoids using the word "love." He reserves the term to describe God's relations with Christ's disciples. Even in the present text he does not leave divine love for "the world" unqualified: the advances of God's love call for correspondence on man's part. Without that response divine love will not, or cannot, realize its designs. By corresponding, man allows God's love to bestow upon him eternal life (v. 16) or salvation (v. 17). By refusing, man rejects the concrete expression of God's love, Christ. John says nothing about God's continued love for those who have spurned his love's advances. In not speaking of God's love for the wicked, he differs from the Synoptics, who hold up God's persistently kind treatment for the wicked, the unjust, and the ungrateful as the model of the Christian's love of enemies (Mt 5:44f.; Lk

6:35). John's limiting his usage of the term "love" in this way has important implications, to which we shall allude later.

Man, then, must respond to God's love so that divine love can achieve its aims. This response is faith: "God so loved the world . . . that everyone who believes . . . may have eternal life." Faith, therefore, which means acceptance of Christ, is acceptance of the concrete manifestation of God's salvific love.

1 John 4 presents faith in the same way but with greater clarity. Verse 9 reads: "In this was manifested God's love for (en) us: that God sent his only-begotten Son into the world that we may live through him." Christ's coming to save us is, therefore, the great and unique manifestation of God's love for us. After the brief development of another idea, John sets about explaining how man accepts the offer of God's love in Christ. "The Father has sent the Son as Savior of the world. If anyone confesses that Jesus is the Son of God, God dwells in him and he in God" (vv. 14f.). In other words, by confessing Christ as the Son of God come into the world, i.e., by accepting him as God's revelation and offer of himself to men, man comes to share God's intimacy: "God dwells in him and he in God." This "confession" of Christ is, of course, faith. Since faith means acceptance of Christ and Christ is the concrete manifestation of God's love for us, faith means acceptance of God's love for us. However, John does not merely let us draw this conclusion for ourselves. He states explicitly: "[By confessing Christ] we have known and believed the love which God has for (en) us" (v. 16a).

Faith and the Love of God

Love of God—John 5:40–44 and 1 John 2:15

After having examined the loves which accompany faith, we may well ask ourselves whether they are not all simply manifestations of love for God. Love for the glory of God, in the sense of readiness to accept a share in God's life which will glorify him, seems nothing other than benevolence or love for God himself. Love for Christ as God's manifestation and offer to men of a share in his glory amounts to love for God who reveals himself in Christ. John himself actually presents the "love of God" as being the ultimate explanation of these loves which accompany faith. The phrase occurs in his Gospel in 5:40–44. The genitive is, of course, ambiguous. The love *of* God can mean *God's own* love (with which God himself loves), love *from* God (come from or given by God), or love *for* God. Since John seems deliberately to avoid the more natural and unequivocal verbal phrase "to love God," his use of the noun phrase bears investigation.

Christ declares the Jews' rejection of himself a proof that they do not have the "love of God" within them. "I know you," he tells them, "that you do not have the love of God in you" (Jn 5:42). The proof follows: "I have come in my Father's name, and you will not receive me." If they had the "love of God," they would accept him and show interest in the glory of God (v. 44). Since acceptance of Christ and especially concern over God's glory imply benevolence towards God, we would naturally tend to interpret this love of God as love *for* God. The only reason for hesitating is the somewhat unusual expression. John could easily have said, "You do not love God." He preferred, "You do not have the love of God in you." This somewhat awkward construction with the genitive seems all the more unusual in view of the fact that the noun *agapē* occurs with relative rarity in the fourth Gospel. Besides, John speaks of the disciples' loving God (using the verb with direct object) in only one place in the whole of his writings (1 Jn 5:2), the climactic passage which explains the full depths of his concept of love. We may wonder, therefore, whether he does not here deliberately choose a somewhat ambiguous circumlocution in order to reserve the unambiguous expression for then. Perhaps he wishes to imply to his readers that his thought has deeper meaning than the merely obvious sense suggested by the context.

The "love of God" reappears in 1 John 2:15: "If anyone loves the world, the love of the Father is not in him." Here, as in John 5:42, it stands in unequivocal opposition to love *for* the world. But here too John expresses his meaning by the same ambiguous phrase: "the love *of the Father* is not in him."

Conclusion

In Christ God offers himself to men out of love. Christ is the concrete manifestation of God's love in the world. To believe in Christ means to accept him as God's offer of himself; in other words, it means to comply with the advances of God's love. Those who love themselves inordinately, who desire a glory independent of the borrowed glory they can have from God in Christ or who love the evil which they have apart from God, can only reject the offer of God's love and refuse to believe. Only those who love God's glory and who therefore love Christ, the manifestation and offer of that glory, will accept the advances of God's love. These are the men who have the "love of God" within them.

ECUMENICAL EPILOGUE

JAMES M. GUSTAFSON

Dialogue on the Moral Life

One gets the impression that while the conversation between Catholics and Protestants has begun to achieve maturity in biblical studies and systematic theology, in the field of ethics it has barely begun. This statement needs explanation. Certainly in areas of practical social action there has been mutual recognition of each other's work in race relations and other problems. On specific questions, such as nuclear war, there has been common participation in conferences. On the issues of Church and State specialists have known each other's work. Other modifications of the opening sentence could be made. But as a discipline of academic study that moves between theology, biblical studies, and philosophy, as well as toward the practical reasoning of moral judgments and actions, not much has been done.

Catholic Moral Theology and Protestant Ethics

Among the many reasons for this I would like to cite two. The first lies in the place that moral theology has had within the theological disciplines of Roman Catholicism. Moral theology has become a

Reprinted with permission from *The Ecumenist*, 3, 5 (July–August 1965). Dr. *James Gustafson* is professor of Christian Ethics at Yale University and author of *Treasure in Earthen Vessels*.

highly specialized and technical science in Roman Catholicism, and in many respects has isolated itself from systematic theology, biblical studies, contemporary philosophy, and other areas of theological research. The Protestant reader of the Roman Catholic textbooks of moral theology finds Scripture used to proof-text affirmations made on non-biblical grounds. He finds admirable acuteness in detailed moral argumentation, but no questioning of some important basic premises of the arguments. He is impressed by the competence of the moral theologians in handling the details of questions of medical ethics and other things, but senses little of what he cherishes as Christian freedom and love for persons. Indeed, many Protestants have written off Roman Catholic moral theology as legalistic hair-splitting based upon philosophical assumptions that can be radically questioned, and armed with such ecclesiastical authority that there is no point in trying to start a conversation. But a less severe judgment is in order. As moral theology frees itself from its academic isolation and begins to take seriously the contemporary Catholic and Protestant biblical studies, the new movements in fundamental theology, and the rethinking of philosophy, both its style and its mood alters, and conversation becomes fruitful.

In contrast to the isolation of moral theology, Protestant ethics has had a different location among theological studies. European Protestant ethics, for example, has been a subsection under dogmatics, which in turn has been closely related to exegetical work in Scripture. In the theology of Karl Barth, for example, one finds major sections under the doctrine of God, the doctrine of creation, and the doctrine of reconciliation that deal with ethics. In each case one is given certain implications from the fundamental theological position for the work of ethics. Indeed, in the case of Barth as well as some Lutherans, one of the implications is that ethics as a science does not have an autonomy to deal with moral questions in the manner that is assumed in Catholic moral theology. Often the ethician finds only a general posture or direction for his work, and certainly little of the precise reasoning about particular moral issues found in Catholic moral theology. He reads about Christian freedom, Christian love, the concreteness of the command of God, but finds little about how that freedom and that love are to be directed and restricted in expression. European Protestant literature shows a serious involvement in what biblical scholars have been saying, not in the explication of the specifically moral statements given in the Bible so much as in the biblical understanding of what the Christian life is. The weak-

ness in this approach is the consequent failure to develop ethics as a
discipline in its own right, and the revision that ethics undergoes
frequently with changes in the consensus of theological and biblical
opinion. Certainly technical competence in the practical science of
casuistry is rarely found, since casuistry itself seems unbiblical and
legalistic.

The American Protestant ethician has had a more practical orientation than his European colleagues, and is usually judged to be
theologically and biblically ignorant by them. The conversation
partners of a man like Reinhold Niebuhr, for example, have been
political philosophers, social policymakers, and social historians almost as much as they have been biblical scholars and theologians.
Since the beginning of the Social Gospel movement almost a century
ago, American Protestants have written much about general economic questions, international relations, race relations, and other
such topics. But this is not moral theology in the Catholic sense.
The absence of serious work in the issues of medical care, with the
exception of Joseph Fletcher's *Morals and Medicine,* indicates the
difference in the direction of practical interests. The fact that the
Niebuhr brothers are at least as important for the development of
theology in American Protestantism as they are for ethics indicates
that even on these shores ethics and theology have never been isolated from each other.

Differences of Approach

The second reason for the difficulty in the conversation between
Catholics and Protestants that I would cite is the Protestant failure
to understand the role of moral theology in Catholic life. Since the
Protestant parson is not occupied with hearing confessions, except
the general confession of a deeply rooted undifferentiated sin, he
has never needed anything to guide him in assessing the degrees of
moral right and wrong. Neither he nor his parishioners have been
trained to grade their sins according to species, nor to tabulate their
number. Protestants usually do not know how closely the manuals
of moral theology are tied to the priest's work as confessor, and thus
miss an assumption that every Roman Catholic priest takes so much
for granted that he never has to state it.

The Protestant ethician has tried to say something important and
influential to the Christian community and to the wider public prior

to an action. Catholics also have been concerned with moral counsel and moral nurture, and have sought to affect general public opinion. But Protestant ethicians have been uninterested in trying to judge the seriousness of a sin after an action has occurred. Except in some conservative, legalistic, and pietistic communions, they have not taken it to be their task to catalogue the "do's" and "don'ts" in the clear and precise manner of the manuals. There is no moral reference bureau or book in Protestant Church life that offers instant wisdom and instant answers to moral questions. The reasons for this are theological and ecclesiastical, and cannot be developed here.

These differences indicate that the basic location, style, and purpose of ethical writing and research in the two Communions are unlike enough to make ecumenical work difficult. The Catholic ethician appears to be working from a relatively stable ecclesiastical culture and institution, with a relatively fixed framework of principles and judgments. The Protestant appears to be working in what one of our own most eminent ethicians, Paul Ramsey, calls the "wastelands of relativism." Some Catholics prize their stability; some Protestants make a virtue out of their openness. Between these two extremes it will be difficult to converse. There are, however, Catholics moving from a relatively fixed and academically isolated closed morality toward more openness both to biblical theology, systematic theology, and newer currents of philosophy on the one hand, and to the situations of persons and the changes of culture and society on the other hand. There are also Protestants who are concerned to give clearer and more precise direction to moral action that is open to the gracious newness of life in Christian love and freedom, and to the new occasions God is making possible in history. In this range of opinion there might well be movement toward consensus. Space permits me only to state, and hardly develop, a few reasons for this assertion, and these only by way of comment on some recent Catholic thought.

Trends Toward a Personalistic Moral Theology

First, within a traditionally Thomistic basis for ethics, there is a renewed emphasis on the virtues, and particularly on the importance of charity and prudence as the virtues that shape particular judgments and deeds. As evidence for this, one can cite Josef Pieper's widely read essay on *Prudence*. In a critical judgment on the practice of casuistry, he writes that it "presents its own kind of peril, owing to that persistent human desire to achieve security." This striving for moral certainty can gravitate "into the degenerate, anti-natural state of nonhuman rigidity. Indeed, this danger is all the greater the more powerfully the desire for certainty is concerned with the decision-making center of the spiritual person." While recognizing that casuistry is a practical necessity, "the immediate criterion for concrete ethical action is solely the imperative of prudence in the person who has the decision to make. . . . The highest and most fruitful achievements of Christian life depend upon the felicitous collaboration of prudence and charity." To the Protestant this and comparable statements are of great significance. The stress is not on rigid dictation by extrinsic and authoritarian interpretations of moral law, but upon *persons* informed by the law of their being and by practical moral reason responding in a manner appropriate to Christian love. Space does not permit a development of Father Gilleman's thesis in *The Primacy of Charity in Moral Theology* (Newman, 1959), with its stress upon love as the form of the virtues in St. Thomas.

Stress on the virtues presents only one way into a more personalistic, open Christian ethics in Catholicism. It operates from within the traditional framework to achieve this end. But the more biblical approach to the Christian life is even more congenial to the Protestant. Rudolf Schnackenburg's recently translated *The Moral Teaching of the New Testament* provides us with a biblical study of great importance to both Communions. While there are some points at which I find internal inconsistencies in Father Bernard Häring's great text, *The Law of Christ* (Newman, 1964), one of its many marks of newness in moral theology is its openness to the New Testament as providing the basic theological and spiritual ground for Christian morality. The *Law* in the title refers not to rigid moral prescriptions, but to Romans 8:2: "For the law of the Spirit of the life in Christ Jesus has delivered me from the law of sin and death." Random quotations from the Foreword are sufficient to show Häring's intention, however compromising it is to the Protestant reader in its execution at points. The Christian life is always to be viewed from the "point of the divine bounty: God wills to give himself to us. . . . In the love of Christ and through the love of Christ for us he invites our love in return, which is a life truly formed in Christ.

. . . Christian morality is life flowing from the victory of Christ, the hopeful anticipation of the Second Coming of the Savior in the glorious manifestation of his final triumph on the great day of judgment." We share in union with Christ, and our imitation of him then is no mere external copying, but a life of love and obedience. The impact of this on the Protestant ethician is great. Biblical theology becomes the ground of moral theology. The life of the spirit, nourished in worship and in faith, becomes an outgoing positive life of love rather than a cramped fear of doing the wrong things. In Christ we have a freedom—from "excessive scrupulosity"—to meet the neighbor's deepest need in love. The person, not the impersonal, is the point where God's work and man's work meet.

There is yet a third movement toward more open and personalistic moral theology. It stems from the impact of the phenomenological movement in contemporary European philosophy. One finds its mark, for example, in Albert Dondeyne's *Faith and the World*, where man's historicity and temporality, and man's freedom are made key points for understanding life in the world, rather than man's determination by some assumed inflexible law of his nature in an almost crude biological sense. Its mark is to be found in the use of the idea of man as responder and therefore responsible, in occasional writings of Robert Johann. In Häring it is expressed as follows: "If religion essentially has the character of response and responsibility, it must follow that an ethic is truly religious only to the extent that it bears the mark of response. The pure type of religious ethic is of the nature of response, in which moral conduct is understood as response to the summons of a person who is holy, who is absolute." Moral life in faith is a life of "fellowship with God," it is speaking and hearing, it is I-Thou communion, it is dialogue. This can be contrasted with the life that seems to be envisaged by the writers of the older manuals of moral theology. There the moral life seems to be one of subjection of the person to the refinements of interpretations of moral laws and to the extrinsic authority of the ecclesiastical institution.

The more personalistic moral theologies place both more initiative and more responsibility on persons. They will rely upon a new understanding of what the nature of a person is. I would conjecture that they also entail a more positive pastoral and constructive relationship of the priest to his people than has sometimes existed, bringing them through the ministry of the Church into a moral maturity that is outgoing, listening to them and working with them in formation of a pattern of life and action that can make them responsive and responsible free persons.

These movements indicate grounds upon which ethicians can join in the interconfessional conversation. Roman Catholicism flirted with "situational ethics" immediately after World War II, and those who espoused this position in a radical way were chastised. There is in Protestant ethics today a lively support of a radically situational ethic, radicalizing the openness of Christians to the world, and relying upon the work of the Spirit to inform the responses of the conscience to a changing world. Some of us begin with a Protestant openness, but seek to find the responsible ways both in theology and in ethical reflection to move between the acknowledgment and joyous affirmation of the "divine bounty" and the responsibilities of serious moral life in the human community. I do not propose that on some nice day, or in some great conference, Catholics moving from order to openness will meet Protestants moving from openness to order, and fall in line together at ease. But an engagement in serious discourse in ethics, as elsewhere, will be to the benefit of each.